ARCHITECTURAL TREASURES OF EARLY AMERICA

★ ★ ★ ★ ★

EARLY HOMES
OF
NEW ENGLAND

ARCHITECTURAL TREASURES OF EARLY AMERICA

★ ★ ★ ★ ★

EARLY HOMES OF NEW ENGLAND

From material originally published as
The White Pine Series of Architectural Monographs
edited by
Russell F. Whitehead and Frank Chouteau Brown

Prepared for this series by the staff of
The Early American Society

Robert G. Miner, Editor
Anne Annibali, Design and Production
Jeff Byers, Design and Production
Nancy Dix, Editorial Assistant
Patricia Faust, Editorial Assistant
Carol Robertson, Editorial Assistant

An
Early
American
Society
Book

Published by Arno Press Inc.

Copyright © 1977 by Arno Press Inc. and The Early American Society, Inc.

Library of Congress Cataloging in Publication Data

Main entry under title:

Early homes of New England.

    (Architectural treasures of early America ; v. 5)
(An Early American Society book)
    1. Architecture, Domestic—New England. 2. Architecture,
Colonial—New England. 3. Architecture—New
England. I. Miner, Robert G. II. Early American
Society. III. The Monograph series, records of early
American architecture. IV. Series.
NA7210.E18   728.3   77-14469

ISBN: 0-405-10068-X (Arno)   ISBN: 0-517-53274-3 (Crown)
Distributed to the book trade by Crown Publishers, Inc.

CONTENTS

17th Century Connecticut

WITH apologies to the author of the famous schoolboy Hibernianism, committed in translating into English the opening sentence of Cæsar, *De Bello Gallico*, we may say that all of early Connecticut was "quartered into three halves." Of these, the first and most anciently settled was the region round about Hartford, including the towns of Windsor and Wethersfield and the tracts bordering thereon. This was in 1636. Not long afterwards—to be historically exact, in 1638—came the New Haven group of settlements, while in 1646 followed the laying out of New London, to which latter sphere of colonizing influence belonged the town of Norwich. There was, it is true, a fourth early plantation (1637) at Saybrook, and on the lands immediately adjacent thereto at the mouth of the Connecticut River; but as this colonizing venture never attained the political nor numerical growth of the "three halves" previously mentioned, and was more or less identified with the Hartford group, we may pass it without further mention here, interesting though it be historically and architecturally, since the houses of the Connecticut River Valley have been discussed.

Our present concern is with seventeenth century Connecticut houses other than those in the valley settlements, or what is known as the Connecticut Colony, embracing the river towns and their offshoots. That means to say that most of our material is drawn from the New Haven settlement, for, thanks to the gentle incendiary attentions of Benedict Arnold, the burning of New London left but little of the seventeenth century work undestroyed in that city. The other seventeenth century structures in the neigh-

boring country are virtually analogous to the New Haven types or else obviously affected by Rhode Island characteristics. Lest the reader be led to expect too great a diversity between the different local types, it is well to preface our detailed examination by observing that, although the "joints visible in the [early] political structure of Connecticut were faithfully repeated in the architecture of the first century of the colony's existence," the differences are not sharp and are chiefly to be noted in matters of detail in such particulars as resulted from "the constructive preferences of the carpenters and masons who literally founded and built the commonwealth, and who, through their successive apprentices, handed down their different craft traditions." The differences are, however, quite sufficient to make study interesting.

The New Haven sphere of influence embraced the towns to the east and west, and the small settlements for a short distance inland from them—Guilford, Branford, Milford, Stratford, Fairfield and their immediate hinterland. Colonists settled in all of these places within a year or two of the colony's planting. And the men of the New Haven Colony were, all things considered, of more substantial estate than any other body of planters who sat down within the boundaries of the present State of Connecticut. They were such men as Governor Theophilus Eaton, Thomas Gregson, the Reverend John Davenport and Isaac Allerton, all of whom had houses befitting their substance and civic importance, while other men of easy means, as affluence was then reckoned, also erected dwellings by no means contemptible. There is also a sufficient number of the houses built in the

THE GOLDSMITH HOUSE, BETWEEN GUILFORD AND BRANFORD, CONNECTICUT.
Built circa 1700.

Detail of Doorway.
THE PHILO BISHOP HOUSE, GUILFORD,
CONNECTICUT.

Detail of Doorway.
THE WALKER HOUSE, STRATFORD, CONNECTICUT.

THE PHILO BISHOP HOUSE, GUILFORD, CONNECTICUT.
Built circa 1665.

immediately succeeding period to give us a very accurate idea of the average seventeenth century Connecticut dwelling. In discussing them we may, for the sake of convenience, follow Mr. Isham's classification of two closely related types of seventeenth century house—the one built prior to 1670 or 1675, and the other built between these dates and the end of the century. One of the chief items of differentiation between the two was the treatment of the lean-to. In the former type it was generally an independent and somewhat later addition; in the latter it was commonly incorporated in the original plan and erected as an integral portion of the body of the structure.

Both types were approximately the same in the contour of their mass—an oblong rectangular main body containing two floors, with an attic in the steep pitched roof which sloped down in the rear almost to the ground, covering the lean-to, and displayed either one unbroken pitch (as usually in the later type) or else a break at the line of junction between the principal mass and the lean-to (as frequently in the earlier type where the lean-to was a subsequent addition), with a slightly gentler slope thence downward; a buxom stone or brick chimney stack rising from the centre of the roof line, the top of the stack capped "with one or more thin courses, which project like moulded bands," and sometimes also another projection or necking below and distinct from the capping; last of all, the overhang, one of the most interesting features from purely architectural reasons and one that vastly contributed likewise to the strongly individual expression of the contour. In the middle of the front was the house door with two windows at each side, while a row of five windows generally filled the front of the second floor, or else there was one window on each side of the door and three on the second floor. From an inspection of the exterior it is possible to form a correct idea of the interior plan. On the ground floor were two rooms, the "hall" or living room, which in the earliest times served for kitchen also, and the parlor. In the middle of the house, between the rooms, was the great stone chimney structure with a capacious fireplace in each room. The house door opened into a shallow entry or "porch." There, opposite the door and backed up against the masonry of the chimney, a stair of three broken flights ascended to the second floor, where were two chambers, with their fireplaces, corresponding to the plan of the ground floor. A stair back of the chimney led from one chamber into the attic. Where the lean-to was a subsequent addition, it contained a kitchen and sometimes a small bed-chamber. A fireplace was added and a flue built up along the back of the original chimney, whose form, above the roof, now became T-shaped instead of rectangular. Above the ground floor of the lean-to there might or might not be a chamber. Where the lean-to, as in the house of the second type, formed a part of the original scheme, its ground plan was the same, but provision was made for second floor chambers, usually on a level with the "hall" and parlor chambers. Ex-

amination of the remaining seventeenth century houses shows that the foregoing simple plan was closely adhered to almost without exception; and when there were any variations, they were trifling.

The framing was sometimes of hard pine, sometimes of oak, and occasionally both were used. It is worthy of note that the framing is still in admirable condition except where it has been subjected to the grossest neglect and exposed to insidious leaks. The exterior casing of clapboards was of white pine, not infrequently left to the coloring agencies of the weather. Man, far more than time or weather, is to blame for the disconcertingly altered conditions that often confront the visitor who endeavors to visualize the pristine appearance of these old houses. The local carpenter of the nineteenth century, who was not an archæologist nor an antiquary and, unlike his predecessors of the seventeenth and eighteenth centuries, apparently altogether devoid of architectural appreciation, reverence or imagination, was the worst offender. If clapboards were to be renewed, he did not scruple to

THE HYLAND-WILDMAN HOUSE, GUILFORD, CONNECTICUT.

THE HYLAND-WILDMAN HOUSE, GUILFORD, CONNECTICUT. Built 1668.
Showing detail of hewn overhang, chamfered girt
and brackets for post at each side of door.

THE BALDWIN HOUSE, BRANFORD, CONNECTICUT.
Circa 1645.

saw off brackets and moulded drops or even wholly to conceal overhangs and chamfered girts if it suited his whim and convenience. Nor did he hesitate otherwise to obliterate sundry architectural refinements that constituted no small degree of the ancient and rightful charm of the seventeenth century dwelling. That so much of the original aspect of the houses illustrated still remains is a matter for real gratulation. Successive occupants, through an ill-considered obsession to follow the latest fashion, have also been much to blame for senseless and regrettable changes. At their instance the external features that suffered the most conspicuous change were doors, doorways and windows.

The original doors, interesting though severely simple, were well considered in composition and detail. One of the earliest doors and doorways may be seen in the Baldwin house at Branford. The frame is simple but vigorous. While door and frame may not be coeval with the building of the house, they are very early, and the square lights, cut in the heads of the three upper panels, are obviously a later "improvement," probably dating from the late sev-

enteenth or early eighteenth century when the fashion of low transoms with small rectangular lights (*vide* the door of the Bishop house in Guilford and others) was becoming popular. It is more than likely that new doors and doorways were installed, in many cases, in the early years of the eighteenth century at the same time that leaded casements were abandoned and the window apertures altered for the reception of double hung sashes. As an instance of this may be mentioned the door of the Bishop house in Guilford: the method of panelling, the moulded capping and the transom of the five rectangular lights are all earlier in type than the date of erection. Again, in the Walker house at Stratford, one is tempted to believe that the door itself and the fluted pilasters of the doorway, along with such elements of a scrolled pediment as are still visible beneath the very much later added porch, were applied when the windows were changed. Time and again both doors and doorways were ruthlessly sacrificed in irresponsible fits of modernism. While eighteenth century alterations, both early and late, were often meritorious, and at least decent, the monstrous nineteenth century

THE STARR HOUSE, GUILFORD, CONNECTICUT.
Built circa 1665.

THE ACADIAN HOUSE, GUILFORD, CONNECTICUT.
Circa 1670.

aberrations of uninspired stock millwork are un-pardonable and revolting examples of proprie-tary vandalism.

All the windows, save those that have escaped the intolerable desecration of recent sashes with large panes, exhibit the double hung sashes with small panes and wide muntins that supplanted the earlier diamond-paned leaded casements in the fore part of the eighteenth century.

Another significant change that seems to have taken place concurrently with the alteration of the windows was the in-troduction of a cor-nice and oftentimes also of moulded barge boards. At first there was no cornice and the only attempt at architec-tural amenity at the eaves seems to have consisted occasion-ally of cutting away the under side of the projecting rafter ends so that they were perceptibly larger at the outer extremity than where they left the plate. Some-times the rafter ends were merely boxed in —if such construc-tion was not original, and it does not ap-pear to have been— as in the Bishop house in Guilford; at other times the rafter ends were sawed off and re-placed by a thin moulded board cornice and the moulding was now and again extended to the embellishment of the barge boards. These mouldings showed great restraint and refinement of profile and are unmistakably of the type be-longing to the early eighteenth century. Exam-ples of these refined cornice additions may be seen in the Baldwin house at Branford, the Walker house at Stratford, where the moulding is also run around beneath the overhangs and breaks out to form cappings for the window frames, and in the Hyland-Wildman house at Guilford, where, in addition to the several other features, the moulded embellishment occurs on the

barge boards as well, by way of a special amenity.

Through the towns of the New Haven region considerable variations are to be seen in the use of the overhang. Sometimes it occurs only on the front of the house. Again, it extends around the sides, as in the Hyland-Wildman house. Still again, there is a gable overhang as well as the overhang between the first and second floors, as in the Walker, Tuttle and Goldsmith houses. At times there is only the gable overhang, as in the Bishop house and the Starr houses in Guilford, while some of the houses, like the Bald-win house and the Acadian house, have no overhang at all. We also find one clearly defined form that is distinctively characteristic of the New Haven locality —the *hewn* as dis-tinguished from the *framed* overhang, the latter belonging more particularly to the Hartford region, the "Connecticut Col-ony," and to Massa-chusetts. An admir-able example of the hewn overhang ap-pears in the Hyland-Wildman house in Guilford. In the framing for these hewn overhangs the posts for their whole height are of one stick of timber. The full size—sometimes as much as 15 inches square—occurs in the sec-ond floor and from this excess of bulk is hewn out the bracket that seemingly supports the over-hang. Below the bracket, the post is dressed down to far slimmer dimensions. With this form of overhang the projection is much less than where there is a framed overhang and there are no turned or moulded drops. The girts were often elaborately chamfered on their lower outer edge and stopped with moulded stops, as may be seen by the illustrations of the Hyland-Wildman house.

From considerations of solicitude for the picturesque in architecture, it is to be regretted

Detail of Doorway.
THE BALDWIN HOUSE, BRANFORD, CONNECTICUT.

THE HOLLISTER HOUSE,
SOUTH GLASTONBURY,
CONNECTICUT.
Built circa 1675.

THE WALKER HOUSE,
STRATFORD, CONNECTICUT,
Built circa 1670.

THE STARR HOUSE,
GUILFORD, CONNECTICUT.
Built circa 1665.

THE HALE HOUSE, SOUTH COVENTRY, CONNECTICUT.

that in many later instances the hewn overhang degenerated into mere lines of slight projection across the faces or ends of houses (*vide* Goldsmith house) and that the hewn brackets and chamfered girts wholly disappeared—a change, however, not at all unnatural in view of the very slight projection originally exhibited by the hewn overhang. Even in its sadly emasculated estate, the overhang has a distinct architectural value. It breaks the depressing monotony of a clapboarded wall, gives an agreeable relief of shadow and imparts a degree of charm that should appeal to the severely practical-minded person in the light of an observation made by a highly successful manufacturer and "captain of industry," to wit, that "beauty is the most utilitarian asset we possess." On the same score we may also address a plea to the hard-headed practicality of the case-hardened utilitarian anent the chimneys, which, with their capping and the resultant relief of contour, line and shadow, are well worth perpetuating to-day.

We frequently hear allusions to the feasibility of developing an American type of domestic architecture. It is too much and unreasonable to expect that any one uniform type of American domestic architecture should ever be arrived at, for we are a mixed people in our varied racial derivations; but it is not too much to expect—rather, it is altogether feasible and logical—that we should hold to and emphasize our historical background by cultivating the types that have grown with the centuries and proved their fitness by long use. The seventeenth century Connecticut type represents a straight, vital and logical process of evolution from English precedent; it expresses locality and racial derivation, and its perpetuation is eminently reasonable and, as proved by centuries of experience, suited to the climate and manner of life of the people.

Another point that commends the early American types to our close attention at this particular time is their simplicity, combined with dignity and adaptability to domestic requirements reduced to the lowest terms. Post-bellum conditions in many places have dictated a far-reaching simplification of domestic *ménage*, and the solution of the problem thus perforce imposed upon us cannot be found in a more appropriate quarter than in the early types that so faithfully reflect the simple but dignified conditions under which our forebears lived.

THE BOSTWICK HOUSE, SOUTHBURY, CONNECTICUT.   Detail of Entrance Porch.

A good example of this type of porch with wood-paneled soffit of the hood.   The seats at the side are modern.

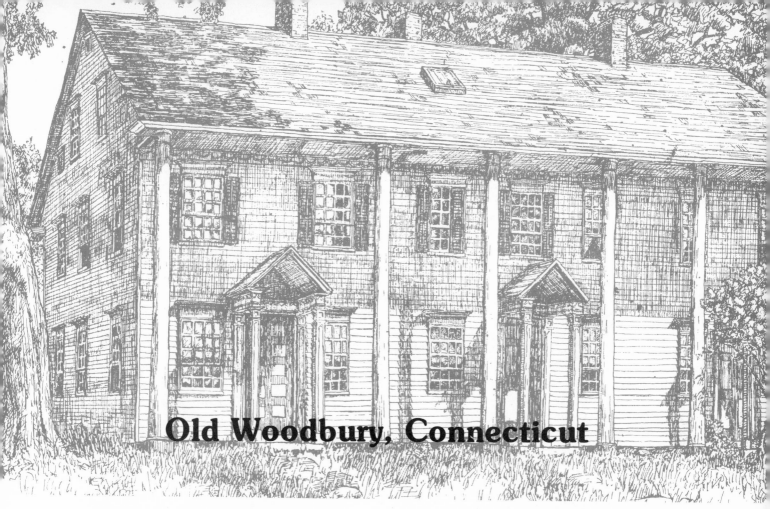

Old Woodbury, Connecticut

THE period of our Colonial architecture does not seem very distant when it is viewed in comparison with the history of architecture of the world, and yet in the short three centuries between then and now great changes have taken place to make our modern architecture a conglomerate mass of uninteresting work. Why this unfortunate development should have been permitted to take place when so many examples of the best of our seventeenth and eighteenth century dwellings remain all about us for our guidance and emulation is a source of wonderment to all thinking persons. The rapid growth of the country both in size and wealth may have robbed us of the desire to express ourselves in terms as simple and sweet as those of our forefathers, but why we should have absolutely lost the spirit of the older homes is hard to understand.

Perhaps if we step back to the town of Woodbury in the pleasant little Naugatuck Valley of Connecticut and picture it at the beginning of our Revolutionary struggles we may gain a concise idea of the spirit that then existed but which unfortunately seems to have long since been snuffed out. If we could have been in this quaint town one Sunday morning long ago we could not help but have become imbued with its atmosphere. It was a clear, bright morning, one long to be remembered by the inhabitants. The British at Boston had already marched out and met the minute-men, and now the men and boys of Woodbury expected to depart in order to join Washington's command, and on

this particular Sunday, just after service at the North Church, a band of men were to leave their homes, some for long periods, others for all time. As the bell tolled in the belfry of North Church, which Hezikiah Platt had designed and built and whose history was to be written in later times, fate decreed that one Jonathan, son of Hezikiah, was here to take leave of Sally Orton, daughter of William Orton. Outlined above the trees the North Church spire stood, dignified, pure white, and delicate of design. In the play of light and shadow, the pilastered front supporting the pediment in which the green blind spread in fan-like shape blended well with the blue and pale yellow facings of the Continental army uniforms so proudly worn by the boys of Woodbury. Sally and Jonathan were wont to take leave, for they were childhood sweethearts, and the Orton house was soon no longer to have Jonathan Platt swing on the picket gate and call to Sally, and then hide behind the stately rose bush that covered its entrance. Just beyond this scene stood the Orton House with its quaint wooden doorway and rough stone door-step, which had served to bind these two. Grown to sweet maidenhood, she had opened this same door for him, for his tap on the knocker was as well known to Sally as his laughter, and if in her anxiety to answer that knock she upset the candle-holder from its lodging place, we can now forgive her for the charred lace work that suffered for her haste. When once inside the stair hall with its stairway of turned balusters and newels, carved scrolls at the open end of

THE SILES HOUSE, LOWER WOODBURY, CONNECTICUT.   Detail of Entrance.

An example of the two-story motif with pedimented entrance which
was employed in Connecticut in the prerevolutionary houses.

the strings, one could see that it was all the work of the elder Platt. Jonathan was ushered into the parlor. Here he could gaze upon the handiwork of his parent by way of a panelled mantel and wainscot, but his gaze rested not long on his father's labors, but upon a pretty face in a poke bonnet, and strange as it may seem, the work of one Hezikiah Platt was no longer thought of. Hezikiah Platt was responsible in his small way for many of the buildings of Woodbury, for he had built for one Abner Lockwood the house at Long Hill where the road turns sharp on its way to Sandy Hook, and the Siles House in lower Woodbury with its pedimented entrance, and then the Judson House, and the Bostwick House, with its simple entrance flanked by well proportioned windows on which the blinds gave a charming color against the white pine clapboards. Yes, the elder Platt had played an important part in the building up of Woodbury, but as things were reckoned then, his houses were but of a type, exemplified by others, similar in design but different in detail, and no one thought but of this kind of house, for had they not all lived the simple life, and why should they not carry out the portrayal of what life was to them in their homes of wood? Beatty Langley and Asher

Benjamin had been their architectural guides, and they could not break from the tradition.

The soldiers from Woodbury left by the post road on this memorable Sunday—left behind all that was theirs, the places their fathers and they had created out of wood and masonry. Shaded streets grew narrow as they passed by the old tavern in the bend of the road where they were lost to view. Over a rise they could still see the North Church spire, quietly nestling in the beautiful valley; and by the church sat Sally Orton, not daring to raise her head, for her very life had gone forth, and Woodbury's youth and manhood, and particularly Jonathan Platt's, were now facing a duty made necessary by oppression, a duty that meant, if well done, the keeping of home and family together—the homes they had built with their own hands, the homes that they had worked for and in which they had taken so much pride. These must stand, must exist, for they were part of themselves. Had not Absalom Turnbull, the village smith, forged the hinges and moulded the knobs of those houses, was not the timber hewn from the clearing and run through the saw by their hands? And so it was that the work of our forefathers, created in mind and mod-

THE ORTON HOUSE,
WOODBURY, CONNECTICUT.

(Home of Sally Orton.)

THE OLD "GLEBE" HOUSE, LOWER ROAD, WOODBURY, CONNECTICUT.   Built in 1771.

The very broad corner boards are paneled on both sides without using a stile and the moulding
is returned across the top.   The first Episcopalian bishop in America was selected in this house.

TWO PORCHES
IN OLD WOODBURY,
CONNECTICUT.

Door blinds add much charm and color to this example. There is something of quaintness and homeliness about these simple blinds.

Rather a good entablature. The triglyphs are not logical in the frieze of a porch of this kind, but are found, however, very often in Colonial examples.

elled in wood, was now to be protected by such men who, going forth to preserve their handiwork, counted not the cost.

This spirit existed at that time, this spirit still exists, but why has the present generation lapsed into a don't-care feeling regarding what home is or can be made? Why do we who sally forth nowadays, familiar as we are with these works of our forefathers, permit the atrocities committed by the so-much-per-yard mills and ten-dollar-per-house, profit-taking contractors? Home does not mean much to these concerns. The pride taken in and thought given to his buildings by Hezikiah Platt do not interest them. Their chief thoughts and interest are commercial ones, and the houses which they produce are usually sad and material examples of what not to do. The beautiful villas with special mention of "Colonial" style advertised for sale by our present day get-rich-quick-build-a-house-over-night realty developers are the blight of our architectural development. How one wishes the word "villa" had never existed, and that it might constitute a crime to desecrate the word "colonial."

This is what we see to-day—this is what the average citizen is buying and building, and,

strange to say, this is what he thinks is beautiful. One wonders what Jonathan Platt, going forth to protect, and Sally Orton, remaining in the background to keep in order for his homecoming the old Orton house with its hollyhocks, foxgloves, and boxwood hedge, with its quiet simplicity, would think if they could view these modern so-called homes. One cannot help but wonder also if the man of to-day has lost the desire for beauty or if it has only been taken away from him by the constant presentation of something hideous. Let us hope that the latter is the case, and that there are numerous Jonathan Platts and Sally Ortons, and that all that is needed for the betterment of our domestic architecture is the removal of the evil manner in which it is created.

Jonathan returns to Woodbury after having served his country well, and Sally is there to greet him. Of course the boxwood hedge is larger, and the rose bush almost hides from view the gate, but all is the same upon his return as far as the house is concerned. The descendants of Jonathan and Sally, taking up where they left off, continued the work of their fathers, for did not the Dennings and Captain Asubel Arnold build according to tradition? Their houses on the bend of the road are pure

Colonial. And until the Greek revival there was no departure from a general type; even with the advent of the Neo-Grec it was so woven into these older creations that no real damage was done, but after this period chaos ran rampant, and as a result we find the nondescripts which unfortunately are with us to-day, the so-called Elizabethan, Gothic and Queen Anne houses with their paper doily edging and verge board scalloping in imitation of pantry shelving paper.

Unfortunately this period acted like a blight on America's architecture, for it fastened itself to the pure examples which fell into its hands, and to-day it is difficult to find a

Detail of Corner Boards.

THE JABES BACON HOUSE, WOODBURY, CONNECTICUT.

In this example a bead takes the place of a stile between the panels. The panel mould miters with the lowest member of the overhang mouldings.

house, either old or new, which is free from its ravages.

It is with a great deal of inward satisfaction and pleasure, however, that we note that the descendants of Jonathan and Sally are again rising to meet and prevent such conditions from going on unchecked. To-day there is a refreshing influence at work in our midst for the construction of houses for these descendants. A new Jonathan Platt and Sally are taking up the work where the former left off. Our architecture is assuming a definite character, and surely will be benefited by the careful study being made by this new generation of architects, who are delving into the beauties of

THE JABES BACON HOUSE, ON THE LOWER ROAD, WOODBURY, CONNECTICUT

One of the earliest Woodbury houses of the double overhang type. The clapboards are fastened by boat nails left clearly exposed and painted over. The porch is of much later date.

Photograph by Lewis E. Welsh

THE SANFORD HOUSE, LITCHFIELD, CONNECTICUT.

OLD HOUSE AT RIDGEFIELD, CONNECTICUT.
The lines of the porch roof have been softened by a very happy treatment.

OLD SLAVE QUARTERS
OF THE BACON HOUSE,
WOODBURY,
CONNECTICUT.

This building is now used
as a tea house.

THE MARSHALL HOUSE,
WOODBURY, CONNECTICUT.

The wing is the original house and is
over two hundred and thirty years old.
The row of two-story columns of
the living-porch is characteristic of
this section and a pleasing method
of handling the piazza problem.

THE BOSTWICK HOUSE,
SOUTHBURY, CONNECTICUT.

The fenestration is excellent for a small
house and the detail of cornice and
window trim very carefully designed.

THE LOCKWOOD HOUSE, CROMWELL, CONNECTICUT.

The main house is over two hundred years old. The gambrel-roofed ell composes nicely with the single-pitch roof of the house.

the older examples, obtaining in their work those qualities and that spirit of quaintness known as America's gifts to the architecture of the world, which have been so long neglected by those responsible for our domestic architecture. This Colonial architecture of our forefathers is again about to come into its own; indeed, there are to-day many instances where we may discover work which is faithful in every way to the best of our early traditions. There is a reversion to a consideration of those subtle qualities which produced the many homes of past centuries that possess a charm that age alone cannot give, but which is the result of that true art of the Colonial builders whose lives were expressed in the design of their dwellings. It is to be hoped that this interest which is being manifested in the best of the old examples of house-building will prevent any further spread of past building evils. That these evils can be removed is certain, but it needs the sincere and untiring help of every one, both in the profession and out. Cosmopolitan America can and should develop a type, and that type may readily have the Colonial traditions as a basic principle.

HOUSE NEAR SANDY HOOK, CONNECTICUT, ON THE SOUTHBURY ROAD.

Typical of the early eighteenth-century houses of the lean-to variety in this section. The windows are divided into twenty-four lights. The original gutters were of wood.

HOUSE ON THE LOWER ROAD, WOODBURY, CONNECTICUT.

THE SHELDON HOUSE, LITCHFIELD, CONNECTICUT.   Built in 1760.
Detail of Entrance and Front Façade.

An interesting minor detail is seen in the device of relating the central projection to the main
walls by carrying the entablature of the colonnade over the first story window-heads.

Litchfield, Connecticut

THE poets have said it, and it is true, eternally true—the hill-man turns ever to his hills, and the mariner ever to his seas. And it is with the same instinct that a New Englander turns ever to New England, and finds it as dearly familiar, as much a place of old and known abode as it is essentially different from any other part of the United States.

This one feels with a peculiar intensity on coming back to New England, after some years away. Gray stone walls, old orchards, spreading elms—and always the good, quiet, unpretending houses of other years. The stranger says that New England is austere, even forbidding; but to the New Englander it is ever gentle, ever welcoming. Gray skies, the soft mantle of sea fogs near the coast, the simple oldness and the spirit of quiet and sincere times, these blend themselves, in some way, into a thing that is the spirit of New England.

A typical New England village, founded before the Revolutionary War, and reaching the zenith of its development in 1830 or thereabout, is like no other place in the world. It is a reflection, in contemporary terms, of the lives and ideals of the people who built it; and because of this fact it possesses, in its very essence, qualities of simplicity and sincerity which, to-day, we find difficult immediately to comprehend or appraise.

There are many such villages scattered through the New England States, from Connecticut to Maine, and many smaller villages, remote from the railroads, sleep beneath their overarching elms, "the world forgetting, by the world forgot."

Although Connecticut is the southernmost of the New England States, its atmosphere is distinctly that of New England, seeming to borrow nothing from adjacent New York State. And so strong (even though undefinable in exact terms) is this "atmosphere" of New England that there is much in common between the seaport towns and the inland towns.

True, the seaport towns have incomparable vistas of blue harbors, and the masts of ships seen at the ends of narrow streets, between silver-gray or white-clapboarded houses; yet the same charm, the same spirit that is *only* New England, pervades the old inland villages. Perhaps they are like two tunes composed with the same melody, or two pictures painted with the same range of colors—variations of the same theme.

Among the older inland towns of New England, specifically of Connecticut, one of the most interesting is Litchfield, founded in 1721. The village, as it appeared at the beginning of the next century, would have seemed, to the founders, a splendidly sophisticated place, an eminently satisfying crowning of their first rude endeavors. To realize clearly just what the Litchfield we see to-day actually means, its pleasant, spacious houses, its serene dignity must be set before a background of the epic simplicity and ruggedness of its pioneer beginnings. And so, a few paragraphs of history, of what is really the epic history of many a similar settlement in New England.

As early as 1715, one John Marsh, a citizen of Hartford, was sent to explore the "Western Lands," as they were called, and he set forth, with a horse and a flint-lock musket, through the trails of trappers and hunters. Thus the spot that was to become Litchfield was found—a beautiful spot, with lakes and timber and good farm lands, and a deed of land was duly bought from the Indians for fifteen pounds. Three years later the land was partitioned into holdings for the charter settlers, fifty-five in number, under Deacon John Buel of Lebanon and John Marsh of Hartford, and in 1721 the village was definitely founded and named Litchfield. Possible error of a clerk is supposed to account for the letter "t," which is not used in the spelling of Lichfield, England, after which the Connecticut village was named.

The pioneers were agriculturists, and the first industries were the grist-mill, sawmill and blacksmith shop; the first tradesman, a clothier. The grist-mill, it seems, was distinctly a community institution, and while farmers waited for their bags of corn to be ground, they read notices of town meetings posted on the door of the mill, gossiped, traded, and indulged in theological discussions which, if not profound, were at least intense and heated.

For many years the safety of the little group of settlers depended upon scouts ever watchful of the movements of surrounding Indians, whose war-dance yells could be heard on the distant hills, while their signal fires gleamed on Mount Tom. In the midst of these perils, and un-daunted by their daily hardships and primitive equipment, the founders of Litchfield gradually evolved the beginnings of the peaceful and comfortable village of later years. Their hardships, their toil, their achievements—these are so stimulating to the imagination that one is reluctant to turn the page.

The oldest house now standing in Litchfield is the Wolcott house, on South Street, built in 1753 by Oliver Wolcott, one of the signers of the Declaration of Independence, and sometime governor of the State. It was in this house that Mr. Wolcott entertained General Washington and Lafayette.

Architecturally, it represents one of the least pretentious as well as one of the most typical examples of the early New England dwelling. The inland towns and villages of New England being, for the most part, less prosperous than the seaport towns, less elaboration in architectural detail is found. Not only were the traders and ship-owners of such towns as Salem and Newport more well-to-do than the struggling settlers who depended upon the land for their livelihood, but in the seaport towns there was available far more talent among artisans. This talent is particularly apparent in such coast towns as Nantucket and the towns on the coast of Maine. Most of the beautiful and often intricate carving and moulding of the old doorways of these towns was the work of skilled

THE GOVERNOR WOLCOTT HOUSE, SOUTH STREET, LITCHFIELD, CONNECTICUT.
Built in 1753.
The unusual moulding detail of the pediments over the first story
windows is shown in a special illustration.

AN OLD STORE BUILDING,
LITCHFIELD, CONNECTICUT.
Built in 1781.

Originally located on North Street.
The bowed "show windows"
with the long hood above suggest
distinct possibilities for adaptation.

THE SEYMOUR HOUSE,
LITCHFIELD, CONNECTICUT.

(Now St. Michael's Rectory.)

33

THE W. H. SANFORD HOUSE,
LITCHFIELD, CONNECTICUT.
Built by Dr. Alanson Abbey
about 1832.

THE SEYMOUR HOMESTEAD,
LITCHFIELD, CONNECTICUT.
Built in 1807.

THE BUTLER HOUSE,
LITCHFIELD, CONNECTICUT.
Built in 1792.

Entrance Detail.
THE SEYMOUR HOMESTEAD, LITCHFIELD, CONN.

Front Door.
THE HUBBARD HOUSE, LITCHFIELD, CONN.

THE SANFORD HOUSE, LITCHFIELD, CONNECTICUT.
Built in 1771.

THE TALLMADGE HOUSE, LITCHFIELD, CONNECTICUT. Built in 1775 by Thomas Sheldon.

carpenters and carvers, who were enabled, during inclement weather, to spend months of labor upon the embellishment of the better houses.

Fortunately for those of us who would study and admire their craftsmanship, the vigor and often the unstudied genius of their designs, the wood preëminently used by early American builders was seasoned white pine. This wood, often unprotected for years from the hard New England winters, has survived unimpaired. Whether or not they gave thought to its long endurance, it is certain that those early artisans used white pine because of its ready response to the tool, and its adaptability for delicate and elaborate mouldings.

An interesting and unusual moulding detail is seen in the pediments of the first floor windows of the Wolcott house—a mitered break which was a favorite device of early American wood-workers.

Opposite the Wolcott house, on South Street, stands the Reeve-Woodruff house, built in 1773 by Judge Tapping Reeve, who founded here in 1784 the first law school of the United States.

Litchfield has also the distinction of having seen the foundation (and flourishing success) of the first "female seminary" or finishing school for the more advanced education of "young ladies."

A picture of the village of that time enlivens the imagination, and throws something of the glamour of romance over quaint, elm-shaded Litchfield:

"Imagine these now quiet streets, with red coaches rattling through them, with signs of importer, publisher, goldsmith, hatter, etc., hanging on the shops, with young men arriving on horseback to attend the Law School, and divide their attention between their studies of the law and studies of the pretty girls of the 'Female Academy.' Then there were some gay bloods from the South, so much at home in the town that they disported themselves in pink gingham frock-coats."

So said an eye-witness. Whether or not the pioneers would have quite approved of the sartorial dandiness of pink frock-coats we know not, but it is certain they would have been proud indeed of the distinction which the two schools conferred upon Litchfield, making it unquestionably the intellectual and cultural center of the vicinity. Litchfield's paper, the *Monitor,* in 1798, speaks of the Public Library as having existed for some time, and prior to 1831 the "Litchfield Lyceum" conducted lectures, debates and weekly meetings. So, in making the wilderness to bloom, the old pioneers had not wrought in vain with the forces of nature and the malignity of surrounding hostile Indians.

The main streets of Litchfield, broad and elm-shaded, intersect at right angles, but the street names do not carry through the intersection. There are thus, as the arms of the cross, North Street, South Street, East Street and West Street. Along North Street are many of the most interesting of Litchfield's old houses, rich in that expression of very conservative and self-respecting domesticity that characterizes early New England dwellings of their type.

The house said to be the third oldest in the town was built in 1760 by Elisha Sheldon, whose son Samuel made it into the famous Sheldon Tavern or Inn. The central feature of this house, a very agreeably designed Palladian window, above four graceful columns flanking the door, is a distinctly architectural effort, and was repeated, with variation, in the Deming house, directly opposite, across North Street.

Although the old houses of Litchfield are largely of the same type, they show many interesting minor variations, and in many instances some one detail must immediately delight the

Entrance Detail.
THE W. H. SANFORD HOUSE, LITCHFIELD, CONNECTICUT.
Built about 1832.

discerning eye of the architect. Take, for example, the very ordinary and uninspiring structure of "Ye Old Curiosity Shoppe"—then discover the possibilities of adapting the quaint bowed windows with the long hood above them.

To comment, however, upon the current uses which may be made of the details and devices of early American architectural design, is either to embark upon an extensive book, or to discount the intelligence of the architect. The message is rather one for the restless and ill-humored critic who bewails the fact that we have no "native architecture" in this country, and must perforce (or because of a fancied lack of architectural imagination and sanity) borrow European styles. The fact is, that if we borrow European styles, certainly we do so from choice, not from necessity, and certainly not because we lack a distinctive and very flexible national style of our own. In the range from the great Southern plantation manor down to the most diminutive Dutch Colonial farmhouse, there are houses to correspond with every status existing.

Perhaps there is an increasing general appreciation of the possibilities and variations to be found in the whole range of early American architecture. By an exact application of the word "Colonial," which is more often used very inexactly, there would exist no designation for the first architecture of the American nation, and all work subsequent to 1776 would either be wrongly named, or would exist without a name.

THE REEVE-WOODRUFF HOUSE, LITCHFIELD, CONNECTICUT.
Built in 1773.

Entrance Detail.
THE GOVERNOR WOLCOTT HOUSE,
LITCHFIELD, CONNECTICUT.
Built in 1753.

First Story Window Detail.
THE GOVERNOR WOLCOTT HOUSE,
LITCHFIELD, CONNECTICUT.
Built in 1753.

THE HUBBARD HOUSE, LITCHFIELD, CONNECTICUT. Built in 1833.
Detail of South Doorway.

For this reason, the term "Early American," while a little vague for exact definition, should be more generally used than the misapplied term "Colonial," for it embraces not only all pre-Revolutionary work, but also the whole range of American architecture from 1776, through the Classic Revival, which flourished from 1830 until about 1840, or a little later.

"Colonial," too, is inexact because it recognizes no distinction of locality. And certainly there are wide differences between the early buildings of New England and those of the Southern States, not to speak of the locally characteristic styles of Pennsylvania and those parts of New Jersey and New York States which were first settled by the Dutch.

Most important of all the aspects of early American architecture is the consideration of its general spirit, which seems to make itself felt irrespective of locality or of the specific type or style peculiar to a given locality. Yet this spirit is by no means easy to define, for it is made up of several fundamental traits which are nearly always apparent in our earlier buildings. Above all, early American builders built as well as they knew how, both in terms of design and of material. They did not attempt styles which they did not understand, and they used the most honest and enduring materials available.

Therefore, "style," or "type," did not in the least trouble the builders of Litchfield, and hence the beautiful, unconscious consistency of the place. They were not trying to be clever or ostentatious—they were trying simply to design and build decent, homelike abodes for themselves. As to their success in this—*si monumentum requiris*—there are the illustrations of this monograph, and there is Litchfield itself.

An ancient mile-stone, just outside the village, gives Litchfield as 102 miles from New York City, by the old King's Highway. Not far, yet we should be glad that old Litchfield is not readily accessible. Such places are easily, very easily spoiled by even a little ill-blended modernity. And they are among the most vital and significant of our national possessions—records and reminders of the lives of dignified aspiration and integrity that built this nation.

Let us reckon this one hundred and two miles from New York by stage-coach (leaving, let us say, Fraunces' Tavern), not by motor car, so that we may keep old Litchfield, serene and unspoiled as it was at the end of last century, in the realm of things "far away and long ago."

THE DEMING HOUSE, NORTH STREET, LITCHFIELD, CONNECTICUT.   Built in 1793.

THE PHELPS HOUSE, LITCHFIELD, CONNECTICUT.
The oldest house on East Street, built in 1782.

A HOUSE ON NORTH STREET, LITCHFIELD, CONNECTICUT.
Built in 1785.

HOUSE AT OLD MYSTIC, CONNECTICUT.

Boston Post Road

THE earliest settlement in Connecticut was made not along the shore, but in its center at Hartford. This is rather curious, since the history of all colonization has been that settlements in new countries have been made first at the ports, and have then expanded up the navigable rivers. One would have expected, then, that the first settlements in Connecticut would have been made in some of its many excellent harbors, at New London perhaps, or New Haven or Bridgeport, and that colonization would have spread first up the Naugatuck, the Connecticut and Thames Rivers, and along the shore of the Sound.

But the settlement was made by men from Massachusetts who advanced overland, and, finding fertile bottom land and a smiling soft countryside along the Connecticut River, founded a little group of colonies around Hartford and Wethersfield. The Connecticut shore was colonized not long after, and as trade developed each little coastal town became the metropolis of the farming community in the neighboring back country.

As means of transportation improved, various cities attained positions of dominance, and instead of a dozen or so small metropolises on the northern coast of the United States, Boston and New York became of great importance, while the other cities dropped into subordinate positions, and either grew very slowly, as was the case with New Haven and New London for many years, or actually receded in population, as, for example, Stonington and Essex. These smaller towns became little more than halting places on the famous old Boston Post Road from New York to Boston, but their inhabitants

had already laid the solid foundations of small fortunes, and settling down to a quiet, unhurried life, built for themselves in the closing years of the eighteenth century groups of homes which were in their day of an average quality and cost as high as in any other part of the colonies. Further, since most of the towns have grown hardly at all, and are for the most part beyond the zone of commutation travel to New York or Boston, the houses which served the people a hundred and thirty or forty years ago, have been adequate for their descendants. Where in the big and prosperous cities the proportion of old houses is almost negligible, and the absolute number very few, in the small old towns one could almost fancy one was miraculously returned to the Colonial period, so many old wood-built houses remain.

The settlement was of course by English people, and because the character of the country has changed so little, the names of the towns themselves are a pleasure to hear, recalling visions of old times. The terminology is singularly free from "made-up" names which sound like the titles of a train of Pullman cars; they are all simple English town names, used in tender recollection of the birthplaces of their founders, with one or two reminiscences of Indian nomenclature; and to call them over is to bring to mind the pleasant land of Kent and Sussex and Surrey from which their early settlers came: Westport, Bridgeport, Fairfield, New Haven, Branford, Guilford, Clinton, Saybrook, Lyme and New London—old towns for us, older towns in England.

They are singularly alike even to-day, and must once have been so closely similar that the

Colonial traveller who took the Boston stage-coach from New York to his home town must have been uncertain as to when he arrived, unless he had ticked off the places as he passed. They were as alike as beads on the string of the Boston Post Road,—beads of the same pattern and the same color. Each little town centered around the "green," usually a rectangle nearly square, but sometimes an irregular central space between converging roads, perhaps a long narrow rectangle, or a triangle. Each green was dominated by the church, and the churches, even, were so alike that they offered no convenient means of identification: they were, in fact, often copied directly from others in neighboring towns, as when the trustees of Lyme contracted to have built "a fair copy" of the North Church in New Haven. The stores were hardly distinguishable from the houses, and indeed most shops were only parts of houses devoted to selling things; show windows were uncommon, and those which existed were divided into small panes because it was not yet known how to make large sheets of glass.

The houses, too, were very much alike, simple square boxes, usually two stories in height, with fairly low pitched gable roofs. Occasionally one-story houses with rather steeper roofs were built, and sometimes gambrel roofs were employed on both one and two story houses. The plans showed little variety, being almost always contained in a nearly square rectangle, so that the mass was a simple block, sometimes relieved by low wings, although these were usually later additions. Even piazzas or covered porches did not form part of the original design, so that these old houses depended for their beauty upon two things only: the proportion of a very simple

mass, and the excellence of the sparingly employed detail in cornices, doorways and windows. Pilasters or engaged columns were sometimes used to decorate the principal façades, and sometimes there was a change of material in the first story from that in the balance of the house, but usually the wall surfaces were of clapboards spaced with apparent regularity.

With such simple motives, it is astonishing that the designers could obtain any variety in appearance, and that they were able to make the houses so uniformly lovely. Most modern architects would be put to it were they compelled to work within such narrow limits and with so few opportunities to introduce new motives; yet the old carpenter-architects appeared to be able to produce endless variations of a very simple theme, each worthy of study. Apparently their greatest question was as to whether the front or the gable end should be placed to the street; when the gable end was the main façade they often ornamented it to a degree with them unusual.

Once in a while we find a house which has a plan different from the standard one to a marked degree, and in these the designers evidently felt very strongly the need for symmetry. Take, for example, the Jessup house at Westport; this house has a gable in the center flanked by short wings with hip roofs. Curiously enough neither of the two doorways is in the gable end but they flank it in the wings; and they are by no means as much ornamented as is customary in doorways of this period, but are rather suppressed to accentuate the importance of the central gable end. The extreme slenderness of the engaged columns expresses their purely decorative purpose, and the arches over the windows and the panels below them illustrate very well the way in which

THE JESSUP HOUSE, WESTPORT, CONNECTICUT.

THE JESSUP HOUSE, WESTPORT, CONNECTICUT.

HOUSE AT GROTON CENTER, CONNECTICUT.

45

HOUSE AT GROTON CENTER, CONNECTICUT.

HOUSE NEAR WESTBROOK, CONNECTICUT.

THE JESSUP HOUSE, WESTPORT, CONNECTICUT.

HOUSE AT GROTON CENTER, CONNECTICUT.

HOUSE AT GROTON CENTER, CONNECTICUT.

HOUSE NEAR WESTBROOK, CONNECTICUT.

THE OLD ACADEMY, FAIRFIELD, CONNECTICUT.

THE OLD ACADEMY, FAIRFIELD, CONNECTICUT.

the later Colonial designers used plain surfaces of flush boards as a decoration.

One of the most interesting of the buildings along the Post Road is the old Academy built, as its name indicates, for a boys' school; and its designer evidently felt that its semi-public purpose should be expressed on its façade. This he did by introducing a pediment over the five center bays, and projecting the wall below five or six inches from the main wall. The cupola or lantern is in its present state new, but replaces a former one. The charm of the building is largely in the plain end walls and the flush boards used in the gables and pediment; the detail is not very interesting, but the three doorways, the pediment and the cupola make a quaintly dignified little public building.

New Haven has grown to be a pretty big city itself, but still retains some relics of the time when it was still a toy Colonial city. The old churches still dominate the green, and around it are two or three of the old houses, of type similar to those in the little towns along the Post Road. Going east from New Haven along the road all the way to New London, we pass through an unbroken succession of little towns

which, at least in their central features, have changed little in the last hundred years. We can still form an excellent idea of how Branford, Guilford, Clinton, Saybrook, Lyme and Mystic appeared from the top of the mail stage; or, indeed, from any one of the towns we could know how the others must have looked. Most of them still have at least one old church with four tall columns down the front and an excellent classic tower over the main entrance; the old greens are well kept and filled with old elms, and surrounded by square white houses appearing to regard the green, over the white picket fences which surround them, with an air demurely discreet. Of these houses the several varieties are illustrated: the beautifully placed square old house at Guilford, with its tiny dooryard, shows in its roof of unequal pitches a reminiscence of the seventeenth-century work; the house on the Post Road near Saybrook is as nearly typical of the locality and the period as it is possible to imagine; one of the "early settlers" survives in Groton Center, bearing a tablet which states that "Whitefield the Evangelist preached from a platform erected level with the upper windows of this house, June, 1764." Curious inscription!

THE COUNTY COURT HOUSE, NEW LONDON, CONNECTICUT.

THE STAUNTON HOUSE, CLINTON, CONNECTICUT.

Doorway.
HOUSE AT GROTON CENTER,
CONNECTICUT.

HOUSE AT OLD LYME, CONNECTICUT.

It interests us because of its very humanity, the quality it has of small town gossip. Very likely, not one out of fifty who reads it with edification has the remotest idea of who was "Whitefield the Evangelist," or even a very clear idea as to what an evangelist is or was. The inscription fails to inform us where the platform was erected. Was it against this house, or across the road, or in some neighboring State? And why should this house have been used as a standard of measurement? Yet it is a curiously satisfactory inscription, and one leaves with real pleasure at knowing that the platform was so high, and hopes that the preacher didn't fall off.

Some of the houses are of the humbler sort—farmers' or fishermen's cottages; but all alike are pervaded by the same peaceful spirit which holds the whole countryside in a sort of spell. It must be a very happy life to be a fisherman in the town with the most enthralling name in America,—Mystic; though Qu'appelle in Quebec Province also has its claim. Mystic has not grown at all, but sits on its Mystic River, dreaming of the days when its whale-ships brought back souvenirs from Tahiti and the Marquesas. New London, on the other hand, has grown great, or at least greater than it was, and is fortunate in having one of the few public buildings of Colonial days extant,—the county court house,—from which we gain a very clear conception of what was our ancestors' idea of grandeur. We have advanced beyond them in the understanding of what size is, and what art is, but we can still learn from the quiet dignity of this beautiful old building the value of pure design.

Our ancestors' conception of what was requisite to elevate a building to the dignity of a court house differed from ours, less in the choice of motives than in their size. Pilasters to-day are the things we most commonly use to impress upon the beholder the fact that the building they adorn is one of importance, but where we would

Doorway.
HOUSE AT OLD MYSTIC, CONNECTICUT.

Doorway.
HOUSE NEAR SAYBROOK, CONNECTICUT.

Doorway.
HOUSE AT OLD LYME, CONNECTICUT.

indicate the size of the rooms by running the pilasters the full height of the building, the older designers prefer to superimpose their orders. There are few or no elements we can select from the design of this building which identify it as a public building rather than a residence, and yet its motives subtly express its purpose. The material of which it is composed, the scale of the detail, the general mass and even the lantern are not in any sense distinct from the same motives in private-house work; the pathetic attempts to produce a sense of solidity by the introduction of quoins on the first story and heavy key blocks over the windows are not distinguishing features of this building, or even of other old public buildings.

The same characteristics mark most of the early American public buildings, as for example the New York City Hall and Independence Hall in Philadelphia; the purpose was rarely expressed by magnifying the size of motives, but rather by their multiplication, and it would seem with real benefit to the dignity and quality of their work. A large row of columns is unquestionably an impressive feature, but there seems to be a limit to the size to which they can profitably be used; to increase them beyond this limit is rather an evidence of paucity of imagination than of a lofty conception. It will be remembered that Guy Lowell won the competition for the New York County Court House with a design which was least in scale of all those submitted, and the enormous columns which were the dominating feature of many of the designs submitted became ludicrous when the true scale of the exterior was indicated by Mr. Lowell's drawings. It must also be remembered that there is no problem in classic architecture more difficult than to superimpose orders, especially more than two in number, yet it is a problem which the early architects solved in general much better than we. The greatest difficulty is probably to combine the cornice of the building with the entablature of the uppermost order; certain of our architects have even tried to decorate skyscrapers from top to bottom with applied orders of two or three stories each; it is obvious that it is impossible to reconcile the scale of the cornice of a thirty-foot order with that of a three-hundred-foot building. In this little court house at New London, the two-story building is perfectly terminated with a cornice of excellent scale as regards the order of which it is an integral part.

It is impossible to say just why we are so rarely able to approximate the quality of Colonial work. Certainly we are better educated in architecture,—or should we say *more* educated? We have a wider field of precedent from which to draw and we have more money and better mechanics with the same quality white pine as a building material, yet the Colonial architect showed within his limited field a more daring talent for design, and a greater perfection in execution.

THE CAPTAIN TIMOTHY PHELPS HOUSE, SUFFIELD, CONNECTICUT.
Entrance Detail. Built in 1795.

Suffield, Connecticut

THE villages and towns of New England, elm-shaded, with glimpses of white houses through the green, seem always to have deep roots in our national traditions and consciousness. And New England, too, has associations even more intimate in the minds of most of us, for there are few American families who cannot trace an ancestor who came from a village or town of New England. There is a spirit, certainly, of these early settlers which has widely affected our whole national temperament; New England is our point of departure, no matter how far from its elm-shaded streets many ambitious pioneers have moved and settled.

And it is New England that gives us, as the symbol and type of the American home, the old, familiar "white house with the green blinds." Regardless of the many and varied kinds of houses we build, to satisfy architectural whims, that early tradition of the "white house with the green blinds" is never entirely absent from our thoughts or from our instinctive desires.

New England possesses, in a subtle but compelling way, a complete difference from any other part of the country. Although its spirit is manifest in our national temperament, and in much of our national instinct, New England lies very definitely on the Connecticut side of a State line and New York on the other. The demarcation is almost as distinct as the difference in color on the map.

In Connecticut there are many quiet inland villages and towns which easily escape discovery by the architectural explorer. They are off the beaten track, and have none of the wide familiarity of the well known seaport towns and much visited inland places of Massachusetts and Rhode Island.

Driving from Hartford to Springfield, following the Connecticut River northward, and north from Windsor Locks, the road will run through the old town of Suffield, which was founded in 1670. Proud of its Pilgrim pedigree, the people of Suffield produced an elaborate historical pageant in October, 1920, in commemoration of the settlement, and recalled the dauntless band of Pilgrims who came from Leyden in Holland, whither they had fled to escape persecution in England. Their leader, Major Pynchon, bought the land for the settlement for thirty pounds from the local Indian chieftain, Pampunkshat, and the first Suffield Town Meeting was held in 1682.

A typical bit of New England history, this brief chronicle of the achievement of a group of determined colonists, who turned a wilderness into a town in less than twelve years. They wrought industriously and untiringly with their hands, and must have possessed a will to survive and to progress almost unbelievable in our present era of easy methods and ready-made necessities.

And what, besides their share of colonizing New England and their share in the immortal spirit of New England, did they leave for us to look upon to-day?

The first houses, of course, have disappeared, replaced by their builders and their children as prosperity increased and the struggle for mere existence became less engrossing. One of the

HOUSE AT SUFFIELD,
CONNECTICUT.
Detail of Doorway.

oldest houses in Suffield is the Gay Manse, which bears the date 1742, a sturdy, gambrel-roofed house of the old New England type that followed those earliest ones, in which sharply pointed roof and overhanging second story were features brought directly over from Elizabethan England. Few of that earliest type remain, and relatively few of the first gambrel-roofed New England houses such as this relic.

The Gay Manse is an unusually good example of its type, in proportion, in the contour of its roof, and in the spirit of its detail. The doorway, surmounted by a broken cyma pediment, is in admirable scale with the entire building, and, as a study by itself, reveals no less nicety of scale in its mouldings and parts. The incised "stone joints" of the jambs and lintels suggest the manner of the old State House in Newport, Rhode Island, as well as the graceful pediment, and it is by no means improbable that Newport may have been the source of inspiration. It is even possible that the pilasters, pediments, and mouldings may have been made in Newport, for there were many skilled woodworkers there whose doorways and mantels are found throughout Rhode Island. Be its origin what it may, it is a fine doorway, perhaps the most perfect, architecturally, in all Suffield.

Along the shaded main street there stands another gambrel-

THE GAY MANSE, SUFFIELD, CONNECTICUT.   Built in 1742.

Detail of Window.
THE GAY MANSE,
SUFFIELD, CONNECTICUT.

Detail of Doorway.
THE GAY MANSE, SUFFIELD, CONNECTICUT.

THE THOMAS ARCHER PLACE, SUFFIELD, CONNECTICUT.

roofed house, known to have been built about 1736 by Captain Abraham Burbank. It is a little more pretentious than the old Gay Manse, more elaborate in its detail. It has wooden quoins after the manner of many of the finer houses of Salem and Newport. The main cornice is elaborated with block modillions and the first-story window-heads are elaborated with a moulded entablature, with dentils, and a convex frieze. Two entrances afford further opportunity for studying detail. The first is a plain pediment porch, on Tuscan columns, with a triglyph frieze, apparently older than the entrance in the wing, which has a pediment over a fanlight, on Composite columns and side lights. The treatment of the entablature of this second door, however, is identical with that of the windows, which contradicts to some extent the theory of its later date. The entablature, of course, could have been copied, or, if both doors actually were built at the same time, there is nothing in precedent to say that it would have been impossible for one to have been designed

Detail of Window.
THE HARVEY BISSELL HOUSE,
SUFFIELD, CONNECTICUT.

Porch Detail.
THE HARVEY BISSELL HOUSE,
SUFFIELD, CONNECTICUT.

THE HARVEY BISSELL HOUSE, SUFFIELD, CONNECTICUT.
Built about 1815.

EARLY GAMBREL-ROOF HOUSE, SUFFIELD, CONNECTICUT.

KENT-HARMON HOUSE, SUFFIELD, CONNECTICUT.

with Tuscan and the other with Composite columns.

The wing to the left is apparently a later addition, but even the Dutch Colonial appearance of its roof does not detract from the essentially New England look of the Burbank house. It is a typical example of its style, conservative, dignified, and very expressive of simple domesticity.

The third gambrel-roofed house illustrated is the Thomas Archer Place, built about 1795. It is a far more modest affair than the Burbank house, but offers a considerable architectural enigma. The location of the two doors by no means suggests a rational plan within, and the doors themselves seem to be a part of some much more pretentious house. The door on the end with no steps or approach, or any other apparent reason for being so strangely placed, is in itself a distinguished piece of design, beautiful in detail and exceptionally fine in proportion. The entablature of this doorway, as well as that of the windows, is very similar to the window entablature of the Burbank house, and its date of building must fall nearly in the same year.

Another half-century saw marked differences in the Suffield citizens' idea of a suitable house. Again the name of "Gay," this time in the local designation of "Gay Mansion," built by Ebenezer King in 1795. Much more sophistication is evident; the builder was by no means unfamiliar with the "grand houses" of Salem and Newburyport.

An architrave and frieze make, with the cornice, a complete entablature, which carries around the building, and tall paneled pilasters, two stories high, support it. The main evidence of a greater sophistication is seen in the Palladian window, which was evidently so highly regarded by the builder that he was inspired to somewhat destroy its scale and importance as a feature by making a very much smaller one in the pediment, where there was only room for a fanlight. Both entrances are very like the second doorway of the Burbank house, and there is also practically an identity in the architraves of the windows on the first floor. This whole house, substantially four-square and dig-

nified, is "New England" architecturally personified.

A third type of roof is seen in the Captain Phelps house, also built in 1795. It is the plain "barn roof," the characteristic Connecticut roof, of which so many are to be seen. The Phelps house acquires dignity by means of the tall corner pilasters, and centers its architectural interest mainly in its porch and Palladian window. The porch is a simple Ionic one, with interesting mouldings in its entablature and pediment. The Burbank house would seem to have set a style in window-heads, for here, again, are the same convex frieze and the same mouldings.

The Charles Shepard house is distinguished by its very graceful porch, of which the balustrade, however, would appear to be a later addition. The general proportions of this house, and especially the pitch of the roof, are distinctly of Connecticut.

Another interesting house (again with the Burbank house window-heads) shows a quaint delusion on the part of its builder, who evidently believed that if one porch is desirable, two would be doubly so, which led him to pile one on top of the other. The effect is not a happy one, and destroys the unity which the street front would have if the builder had not been so mistakenly profuse. This house, built by Harvey Bissell in 1815, eighty years after the Burbank house, also has rusticated wooden quoins, and, as above mentioned, the same win-

THE CAPTAIN ABRAHAM BURBANK HOUSE, SUFFIELD, CONNECTICUT. Built about 1736.

dow-heads. The porte-cochère at the left is very evidently an addition of the "Chamfered Corner" period of the '80's. In 1812 gambrel roofs had given place to the plain "barn roof," but the device of carrying the clapboard side walls down to the grade with no foundation exposed is a much earlier and very characteristic New England custom.

There is an interesting quality in nearly all the early houses of Connecticut which differentiates them from those of other parts of New England, especially from the Massachusetts houses near Boston and the Rhode Island houses near Newport and Providence. The early Connecticut builders were very unsophisticated, and worked with far less actual knowledge of architectural detail than many of their contemporaries elsewhere. It is easy, for this reason, to find many mistakes and solecisms, but these seem more often to add interest to than to detract from their work.

Architecture in the United States enjoyed, in its early days, certain advantages which do not exist to-day. Natural limitations of stylistic influence existed, and while many may think of Colonial and early American builders as de-

Palladian Window.
THE GAY MANSION, SUFFIELD, CONNECTICUT.

prived of the many sources of inspiration which are available in this age of photography and printing, they are to be congratulated on having less distraction. The very limitations of their architectural knowledge made for a fundamental quality of consistency in their works.

A relative limitation which further aided the consistency of builders' and architects' work in the early days of this country lay in the natural limitations of manufacturing mouldings and ornamental detail. Similarity of ideals and the primitive state of mill machinery made for a natural simplicity which to-day is only the result of conscious study and effort. To-day we try to keep our detail simple by referring back to early American work; the early American architect, who was also carpenter and builder, kept his detail simple because he did not know any other kind, and could not have gotten it made if he had known.

Practically every detail was derived from one of the few available books of the time, and these books, for the most part, contained only good and consistent Georgian details. It is interesting to notice in many

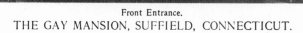

Front Entrance.
THE GAY MANSION, SUFFIELD, CONNECTICUT.

THE CHARLES SHEPARD HOUSE, SUFFIELD, CONNECTICUT.
Built in 1824.

Porch Detail.
THE CHARLES SHEPARD HOUSE,
SUFFIELD, CONNECTICUT.

New England towns how successive builders conferred the highest form of flattery upon neighbors and fellow-townsmen by imitating some detail which seemed attractive. The treatment of windows in the town of Suffield will be observed from the illustrations to show this imitative tendency. Whether executed by the same builder or by different builders, it is apparent that a good piece of detail was appreciated and duplicated in successive houses.

There were stylistic fads in those days, too, but they differed from our stylistic fads in that they came in waves, and not all at once, as ours do. There was, for instance, the Classic Revival, also called the "American Empire," style, which came in after 1812—but the architects, builders, and owners in early American days did not have to worry about Italian villas, French châteaus, English country houses, and California Mission houses all at the same time. They concerned themselves only with the thing that was engaging popular fancy at the time, and even more often they concerned themselves only

THE CAPTAIN
TIMOTHY PHELPS
HOUSE,
SUFFIELD,
CONNECTICUT.
Built in 1795.

with immediate local precedent. It is this latter circumstance that makes the old New England village what it is—a page of architectural history rather than a page out of an architectural scrap-book.

Besides the natural similarity in stylistic inspiration in the average New England village, their charming consistency was further aided by a general similarity in building materials, and the difficulty of securing materials alien to the immediate locality.

And, whatever may have been their limitations, they all had the inestimable virtue of simple sincerity. The houses which they built were homes, the foundation of our country to-day, and their architecture, because it was a sincere effort toward better things, plays its part in our great national architectural heritage, handed down from the first colonists and the first Americans.

"THE GAY MANSION," SUFFIELD, CONNECTICUT. Built by Ebenezer King in 1795.

THE PRATT HOUSE ON BACK STREET, ESSEX, CONNECTICUT.

THE OLD PARKER HOMESTEAD ON WEST AVENUE,
ESSEX, CONNECTICUT.

Essex, Connecticut

"I remember the black wharves and the slips
And the sea tides tossing free:
And the Spanish sailors with bearded lips.
And the beauty and mystery of the ships
And the magic of the sea."

THERE are no black wharves now if ever
there were, nor slips, and the sea tides
barely reach it; the last Spanish whisk-
erado who swaggered through her streets has
long since been gathered, beard and all, to his
fathers—but as by the perfume of a memory
Essex is haunted still by "the beauty and mystery
of the ships and the magic of the sea." Dreaming by the river, the drone of the motors on the
State highway further back does not disturb her
peace. Her dreams are of that earlier day when
the first Lays and Haydens came to Potapaug
Point and Uriah
Hayden built the
old Ship Tavern
just where the
road which is now
Essex Main Street
came down to the
river and the
ferry to Ely's
Landing on the
easterly bank,
nearly opposite.
It is said that in
Massachusetts the
county of Suffolk
lies north of Nor-
folk county; this
seems so much too
good to be true
that I never in-
vestigated the

authenticity of the report. It is for the same reason that I decline to inquire why Essex is on the
west bank of the river. There was a busy inter-
course between the two banks, for in the old days
the ferry at Old Lyme and the Essex-Ely's
Landing Ferry seem to have been the only regular
means of crossing the river between its lower
reaches and Hartford. There is a legend that
Daniel Webster, on his way from Boston to
Washington, reaching the river after the ice had
stopped the ferry service and before it was strong
enough to bear the weight of a travelling coach,
spent several days
on the easterly
bank in the hope
of a freeze and fi-
nally had to drive
up to Hartford
and cross there—
a tale which
throws interesting
light upon the
leisurely pace and
delightful incon-
venience of travel
in the youth of
this Republic.

It was on Pot-
apaug or Big
Point that the old
shipyards were
(they were burnt
by the British in

THE VILLAGE SMITHY, ESSEX, CONNECTICUT.

THE OLD SHIP TAVERN, ESSEX, CONNECTICUT. Side Elevation.

HOUSE OPPOSITE ST. JOHN'S CHURCH.

THE "COLONEL LEWIS" HOUSE, MAIN STREET, ESSEX, CONNECTICUT.

1812)—on the north side of Essex Main Street. The Lays seem to have been the first owners of the whole point and the Haydens to have bought from them the land on the southerly side. But Haydens and Pratts and Lays intermarried as people will and it is difficult now and quite unprofitable for a stranger to attempt to unravel the rival claims to priority and prestige which the inquiries in even a few hours' sojourn stir up. These Lays and Haydens were all shipbuilders and shipmasters; as a measure of the town's traditions, out of eight male Haydens in one family seven were sea captains. In those days the two bridges down at Old Lyme were not dreamed of— now they seem to be a barrier between Essex and that sea with which she had then so close a tie

THE JOHN PRATT HOUSE, MAIN STREET, ESSEX, CONNECTICUT.

and of which the river mouth was a gateway, the Sound but a vestibule. Not a vestige remains of the old yards where they built the tall clipper ships for the China trade and vessels of lesser tonnage for coastwise traffic; but on a quiet autumn day one has but to close one's eyes to hear the ring of the mallets and to smell the oakum and the tar that stopped the seams of those gallant craft—ships which linked a little village in Connecticut to the Flowery Kingdom and all the fragrant East. It is a haven now for the old cup-defender *Dauntless,* and it was on a quest for her that we made a detour from the high road and first found Essex. Moving swiftly through the streets I received an impression of many curved roofs covering low, snug houses, and I was prepared to

THE OLD SHIP TAVERN, ESSEX, CONNECTICUT.   From the River Side.

account for them by Dutch influence. But not a Dutchman nor a Dutch name was to be found on a second visit, only good old British names like the Lays, the Haydens, the Pratts, the Lewises, Starkeys and Hinghams. Nor could I find more than three curved roofs in the entire town; but for these it is easy to account— one at least was built by a ship- builder, another by a sea captain of a type more sensitive to influ- ences than the rest and who wished to recall ashore the sweep of line of his home afloat. At all events I am prepared to main- tain that in an atmosphere of New England primness these sweeping roof lines are as re- freshing as a breath of the sea— a primness which must have been somewhat miti- gated at times if we may trust the mute witness of a bill of sale to Molly Lay, hung up in the old Ship Tavern, and of which the chief items are rum and gin.

The old Hayden Homestead, the third house up from the river on Essex Main Street, has a hip roof, unusual among its gabled neigh- bors. It seems that up the river at Windsor "they knew how to make such roofs," and there was a carpenter of parts who knew the secrets of cutting rafter bevels and such, and instead of travelling about to do the work stayed comfort- ably at home and shipped the shaped lumber. The roof framing, at least, of this house and pos- sibly the whole frame, was rafted down the river

ENTRANCE PORCH OF PARKER HOMESTEAD, ESSEX, CONNECTICUT.

and one other roof in the village is reputed to have made a similar voyage. There is every evidence of a quiet prosperity in the character of the exterior detail of many of the houses, al- though, except in the Tavern, the interiors are quite without in- terest; not even first-rate chimney- pieces survive. And the town as a whole has suffered from the Greek revival—a Greek with a particu- larly heavy hand appears to have been resuscitated.

Coming up the river or along the State highway be- tween Saybrook and Hartford, you may see Essex— the new Essex— climbing her hill among the trees. And dwellers in the old Essex and the new climb of a Sunday to the four churches whose spires and towers of the most fearful and won- derful design prick through the leafy screen, ugly but picturesque. Around these churches, set quite close together in a neighborly way, quite in contrast with the usual superior airs of withdrawal and isolation churches of differing tenets seem to give them- selves, are inter- esting arrangements of shady levels and of roads ramping up and roads ramping down, altogether distinctive in the atmosphere they create. From this upper level, West Avenue leads over and down to the State road. "Avenue" has a sus- piciously modern sound—and in spite of one or two good old things like the Parker Homestead and one little, old, long yellow house, has little of interest to commend it except the Village Smithy,

THE OLD STARKEY PLACE, MAIN STREET, ESSEX, CONNECTICUT.

ONE OF THE OLD HOUSES ON LITTLE POINT STREET,
ESSEX, CONNECTICUT.

No. 27 MAIN STREET, ESSEX, CONNECTICUT.

THE OLD STARKEY PLACE, MAIN STREET,
ESSEX, CONNECTICUT.

THE LONG YELLOW HOUSE ON WEST AVENUE, ESSEX, CONNECTICUT.

in which the fifth generation of Pratts, a family of seamen and smiths, still follows one of the family callings. The location of the smithy would seem to indicate the importance of this road (or Avenue, as it seems to prefer being called) as the principal connecting link between the river and the high road in days gone by. But although the old Town Hall is well up on the flank of this hill, it is the very oldest part down by the river which means Essex—Essex Main Street, the street next to it called with blunt simplicity Back Street, Little Point Street, where the Old George Hayden house stands and where, opposite, running down toward the river, are three or four tiny, low, one-story cottages, which, taken together, give a very definite charm and character to the street. One of them was built by Uncle Noah Tucker, and Cap'n Charley Hayden has lived in it for forty-two years; he and his brother George in the street adjoining are the last survivors of the Hayden family. Cap'n Charley declares them to be "t' old and t' ugly t' die"—an opinion he would not wish me to share.

However ardent an advocate of progress one may be in theory, it is in towns like this that one regrets its march. Instead of the old coaches lumbering down to the ferry with all the picturesque accompaniments of a stop and a drop at the Tavern, an occasional copy of the works of Mr. Henry Ford (himself, it will be remembered, an advocate of peace and the supercargo of a peace ship), rattles and coughs, shakes with its peculiar palsy and invades the brooding peace of the waterside. Instead of the old shipping of Revolutionary times, trim motor launches and smart small sailing craft mark the difference between sailing as a pastime and sailing as a life to be lived. But as the shadows grow longer and the reaches of the beautiful river begin to draw to themselves the cobweb texture of the twilight, the ghosts of old ships ride on the rising tide and Essex, dreaming still, comes into her own again. It is only in dreams we find our own.

THE "COLONEL LEWIS" HOUSE.

TWO HOUSES ON ESSEX MAIN STREET.

THE GEORGE HAYDEN HOUSE, LITTLE POINT STREET, ESSEX, CONNECTICUT.

DETAIL OF DOORWAY
SILAS DEANE HOUSE, WETHERSFIELD, CONNECTICUT

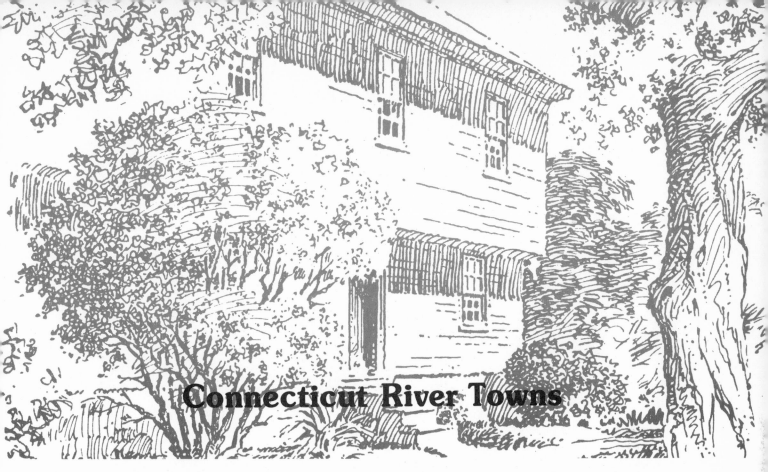

Connecticut River Towns

IN the early days of the Massachusetts Colony, there were a number of the colonists who felt that the district around Boston was becoming too thickly settled for them, as well as that the religious and political attitude of their neighbors was too strict, and accordingly, with what possessions they could manage, little groups set off westward into the unexplored wilderness, without any idea of their destination and with no knowledge of the country, other than various tales of the Indians to be found there. Eventually, these courageous explorers reached the Connecticut River, and there, where the valley invited settlement, not only with water and meadows, but also with exposure to the sun and a pleasant climate afforded by its north and south direction they founded a straggling line of towns, which extended for nearly a hundred miles in length.

Among these towns were Windsor, Hartford and Wethersfield, the so-called "River Towns" of Connecticut. The other groups of settlements in Connecticut were those around New Haven and those of New London. The "River Towns," however, were the earliest, Hartford having been settled in 1636 by Hooker and his group of one hundred emigrants from Cambridge, while Windsor and Wethersfield were established by others from Watertown and Dorchester.

These settlers underwent great struggles for existence during the first years in their new homes; the Indians, who were friendly at first,

soon took to the war path and an almost interminable struggle began. It was also a long way to their base of supplies, a trip by boat around Cape Cod, through the Sound and then up the river, a trip that was fraught with hazards. Accordingly, the first houses that were built, after the period of simple abris which served as preliminary shelters, were quite simple and somewhat crude. The plans were generally of one or two rooms on each floor with a central chimney, and the entry and stairs in the space in front of this. The next step in planning was the lean-to which provided a kitchen and bedroom, but during the last quarter of the century, this became not only a usual part of the house, but part of the original plan. The lean-to was pretty generally abandoned for the full two stories during the early 18th Century, and with the increased depth of the house, the simple gable roof was frequently changed to a gambrel, and the long slope over the lean-to ceased to exist.

During this time, when the typical plan was changing, materials were becoming more plentiful, and undoubtedly the process of building was becoming more familiar, so that larger and more substantial houses were being erected; small "estates" were being established along the broad streets of the towns, the houses at the road, with meadows and farm land extending back in the valley to the foot-hills. With this increasing comfort and security more attention began to be

THE WEBB HOUSE, WETHERSFIELD, CONNECTICUT

DETAIL OF DOORWAY
THE WEBB HOUSE, WETHERSFIELD, CONNECTICUT

paid to the ornamental features of the houses, to the doorways, the window trims, and the cornices, which were executed more or less crudely from the memory of the English work the builders had seen.

It is generally with the houses of this period that the interest in Colonial architecture as prototypes for present-day work begins, and I sometimes think it would be fortunate for modern domestic architecture if our interest had ceased with that period. The widely distributed general familiarity with the later and more ornate forms have lead to the achievement of much "Colonial" work today which is only a collection of tricks, with small scale detail generously distributed, making fussy compositions, regardless of the authenticity of the various elements. To study these 18th Century houses with their simple masses and their decorative features well placed, though frequently crude, is a pleasure, and gives one a sense of the solidity and virility that is essential in real architecture, a sense that even the most untutored layman unconsciously feels and which makes him admire and desire the old houses of New England.

They are typical of the "River Towns" of the Massachusetts part of the valley, and yet they are also typical of the other Connecticut settlements. The other groups, New Haven and New London, did not vary greatly in their political forms from the "River Towns," and neither did they vary greatly in their use of architectural forms. There was the same general plan; the differences were differences of detail.

The house at Windsor is one example where the gable end faces the street, so that practically all of the decorative effect is on this one façade which gives almost a public character to the building. It is one of the later houses, and the detail has become quite accurate, though not over-elaborate. The fence is particularly good in design, adding a great deal to the charm of the composition and becoming an essential part of the design, when the house stands so near the street.

HOUSE AT WINDSOR, CONNECTICUT
Windsor, with Hartford and Wethersfield, formed the famous early "River Towns" of the Connecticut Valley

DETAIL OF DOORWAY
E AT WINDSOR, CONNECTICUT

The Webb House in Wethersfield is best known not only because of its architectural qualities, but because of the historical interest which it bears. It was there, during the time when it was Joseph Webb's Tavern, that Washington and Rochambeau held a council and decided on the plans for the Yorktown campaign. Obscured by the trees in our photograph is an ell which extends behind the main portion of the house and at right angles to it; this was the original early house, with a second story overhang it was moved back from the street in 1750 to allow the larger house to be built. The façade is very well proportioned, and has excellent fenestration; the large windows, with their twenty-four panes, giving remarkable dignity. While the porch, as it exists, may be later, it undoubtedly replaced one of practically the same design and proportion.

THE WATSON HOUSE, EAST WINDSOR HILL, CONNECTICUT

In construction, the Webb House has a certain archaeological interest as it marks the transition in this district from the early to the later method of framing for the floor joists. The left hand portion has the early method where the "summer" runs parallel with the ridge, while the other half of the house, though certainly built at the same time, has the later method of running the "summer" from the header at the chimney to the front wall, parallel with the end walls. The Wareham Williams House in Northford is of the same general type again, but the doorway places it as earlier than the Webb House. This doorway, with the one at Windsor, and the doorway from the Silas Deane House at Wethersfield, are typical of Connecticut Valley work for the first half of the 18th Century. They show clearly that the precedent for applied features was English; the general forms are distinctly English, adapted to wood, while the moldings follow the classic, that is, the classic as debased in the English Renaissance, as nearly as memory and the tools at hand would permit. Crude though they may be, they possess a fine vigor and a sense of scale which is usually appropriate.

Judging from the differences in window trim, it would seem that the Oliver Ellsworth House, at Windsor, is one of the typical houses which was later enlarged. The two chimneys mark the ends of the original house, a well proportioned façade not unlike many others, but with the addition of the two storied porch, and the lengthening of the house, it takes on much of the character of the Litchfield houses, and is rather unique for the "River Towns" district.

The three-story houses which were built in Salem and Providence between 1780 and 1820 are not found much in Connecticut and the Watson House at Windsor Locks is one of the few that were built. The doorway shows a great deal more sophistication and finesse than the earlier work, while the Ionic caps and the Paladian motive over the doorway bespeak a greater knowledge of de-

HOUSE AT ROCKY HILL, CONNECTICUT

HOUSE AT WINDSOR, CONNECTICUT

HOUSE AT WINDSOR, CONNECTICUT

*Types of Doorways
found in "River Towns"*

79

tails and a greater effort at design than is shown in the simpler houses. In the Old Inn on the Hartford Road we see the same attempt to achieve an architectural effect.

The long first story windows in the house at Windsor Hill, shown rather mar the Colonial feeling of an otherwise pleasing elevation. Almost mid-Victorian in their proportion, it is probable that they were enlarged sometime after the original construction. The doorway is extremely interesting, and very much like those on the Stebbins House in Deerfield; the small arched, Palladian-like panes in the transom have a decided Georgian feeling, and form another link in this close relationship between the architecture of the two countries.

In the farmhouse at Rocky Hill, once part of Wethersfield, we find the overhang at the second floor on the front, while on the gable end it occurs at both the second and third stories. This slight overhang was used on many of the houses of the early part of the century, and is all that remains of the greater projections which occur on the 17th Century houses, where they were frequently ornamented with large carved drops. What the origin of the overhang was, is a question that has been much discussed. Some writers have maintained that the large early projections were to afford space for loopholes through which the occupants could offer resistance to attacking parties of Indians or other enemies. This premise, on the face of it, seems somewhat absurd,

OLD INN, HARTFORD ROAD, CONNECTICUT

as the protection afforded would be against only those who had reached the walls of the house.

The most reasonable supposition for the unusual framing would be that the carpenter-architects were using the English methods with which they were familiar. That is, in certain parts of the west of England, there are various examples of timber construction where the overhangs were formed by cutting large pieces of timber down to the size of the corner posts for the first story, and the upper end left larger, forming the projection to carry the posts above. In many cases this was then repeated for the next story as well. In the case of the English work, where the surfaces of this type of construction were generally covered with stucco, these overhangs served the purpose of protecting the walls below from the weather; they also afforded on the upper floors a little more space than was permitted on the street floors. From the fact that we know that certain of the settlers of Connecticut came from those parts of England and that some of the same group were around Ipswich, where the second story overhangs also occur very frequently, it seems quite logical to assume that they were simply following the methods with which they were most familiar.

On our Colonial houses the overhangs were only decorative and were gradually reduced until the projection was only a few inches, or room for a series of moldings, as seen in this example at

THE WAREHAM WILLIAMS HOUSE, NORTHFORD, CONNECTICUT

WAREHAM WILLIAMS HOUSE, NORTHFORD, CONNECTICUT

Rocky Hill. The doorway here has been worked into the projection very knowingly, the moldings lining up with the bed molds of the cornice; but in the case of the doorway at Windsor, the builder solved his problem, breaking trim at the overhang, rather than by trying for an architectural solution.

The difference between the houses of the first part of the 18th Century and the latter part was largely due to the Revolution, and its effects on the general population. Just as in the case of the Great War, building in general was pretty much at a standstill during the Revolution, and afterwards it was found that, while many persons had lost their money, others had accumulated fortunes from the industries that were built up by the war. And so we find that more pretentious houses were demanded. With this general activity came the publication of books, both in England and in America, concerning architectural forms and details, chief among them being Asher Benjamin's "Country Builder's Assistant," published at Greenfield in 1797. These books gave

DETAIL OF DOORWAY
FARMHOUSE, ROCKY HILL, CONNECTICUT

more accurate details of the Classic and Renaissance periods and actually started the study of architecture in this country. Accordingly, architects appeared whose individuality marked their work from that of others, bringing their names with their designs down to the present time.

The study of the Classic forms soon started the Greek Revival, the next step in our architectural development, which, in turn, was followed by the "Queen Anne" cottages and the Victorian era of bad taste. Organized architectural education, both here and abroad freed us somewhat from these "Styles," took us through the French influence of the '90's and brought us to the present period of such complete information that to-day we are able to design in any style the client may request with more or less success.

However, through all this confusion, there still persists a very genuine interest and appreciation of our first American architectural period and for the architect who would achieve the restful simplicity of the work of the truly Colonial times, the simple, well-proportioned houses of the 18th Century will continue to be an inspiration and delight.

A FARMHOUSE,
ROCKY HILL,
CONNECTICUT

A HOUSE AT WINDSOR HILL, CONNECTICUT

DETAIL OF DOORWAY
HOUSE AT WINDSOR HILL, CONNECTICUT

THE OLIVER ELLSWORTH HOUSE, WINDSOR, CONNECTICUT

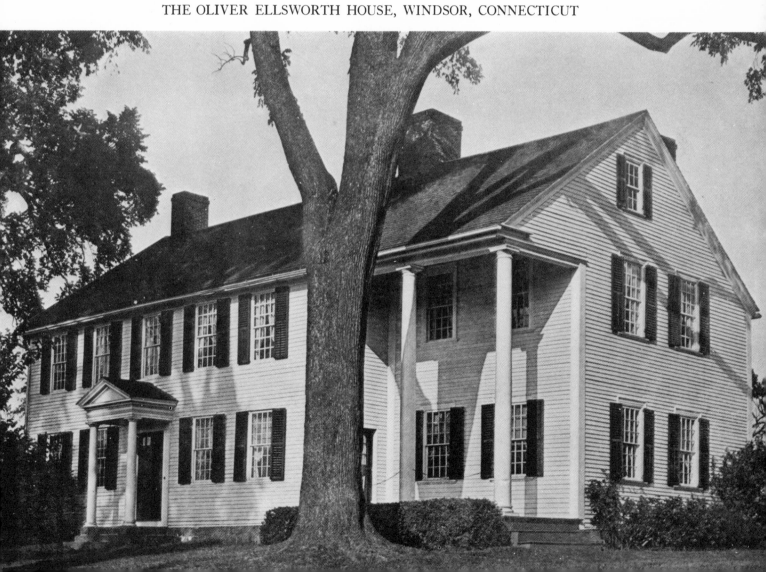

THE BUTLER HOUSE, LITCHFIELD, CONNECTICUT. Built in 1792.
Detail of Doorway on Corner of North and East Streets.

Hartford-Litchfield Stagecoach Road

HARTFORD was the first settlement in Connecticut, an outpost of the Massachusetts colony planted to keep off the Dutch of New Amsterdam who claimed the fertile valley of the Connecticut River for their own. Established in 1636 at a most excellent point near the head of navigation on the river, and in the center of the most fertile part of the state, Hartford early became a little metropolis, from which roads were thrown out to the farming country around it; and as the early settlements grew and became in themselves little centers, Stage Coach lines were established to accommodate the growing travel.

Of these subordinate centers Litchfield was one, although just why the town should have had even local importance, is hard to say. The site of Litchfield is a lovely one, but it is on top of a rather high and steep hill, and the surrounding country is so rough and broken that it could never have been a very productive farming region. Nor were there other industries which could cause growth; there were excellent deposits of iron ore some twenty miles away, and splendid water power at Falls Village on the Housatonic River, near the Massachusetts State line, but though these were discovered and used early in the Eighteenth Century, neither Salisbury nor Falls Village have ever grown very much, while Litchfield was not only a town large by Colonial standards, but a very wealthy little place.

So of the early stage lines, out of Hartford, one ran to Litchfield over the level valley to Farmington, a beautiful old town settled in 1640. The road crosses the Farmington River and continues up the fertile river valley to Unionville, where the road

Litchfield Stage Coach under Shed
OLD TAVERN , DANBURY

THE SHELDON
TAVERN,
LITCHFIELD,
CONNECTICUT

*Built in 1760 by Elisha
Sheldon for a residence
but used as an Inn by
his son Samuel until 1780.
Also known as the
Gould House until 1871*

crossed the river again, and ascended a steep ra-
vine to Burlington. Then came a long stretch of
road along the bottom of a narrow rough valley
to Harwinton and East Litchfield, where the Naugatuck River was crossed, and the four mile steep

climb to Litchfield was begun.

The exact date at which this line was established
is not known, but it was certainly before 1755, and
the line still ran in 1870, when the railroad killed
horse-drawn competition, and the old stages were

THE JOHNSON HOUSE, FARMINGTON, CONNECTICUT
Built in 1690

HOUSE AT THE HEAD OF THE GREEN, BURLINGTON, CONNECTICUT

sold off. They must have built these stages well, for tradition says that some of them were sent to Deadwood, Montana, and that the Deadwood coach which Buffalo Bill used to dramatize was one of them, brought across the continent. Nor was this the only hard usage they withstood, for until the trolley ran to Farmington, the girls of Miss Porter's school were met in Hartford by one of them. This particular coach is still extant and was under a shed of the late Mr. Ives' Colonial Museum at Danbury, as recently as September

of this year, when it was to be sold at auction.

Most of the old stage coach roads, or post roads —they were both—have long since been improved beyond recognition, for generally speaking, the towns of importance a century ago are the towns of importance today; but this old road from Litchfield as far as Unionville remains as it was, and were it possible, some old gentleman who left the Phelps Tavern in Litchfield at six o'clock in the morning, Standard time (it is a misdemeanor to use Daylight Saving time in Connecticut) on August 19,

Doorway Detail
THE BROWN INN, BURLINGTON, CONNECTICUT

1823 he would have found few changes had he travelled with Mr. Whitehead and myself on the same day in 1923. Even the road cannot have been much improved, although he might have been somewhat surprised at the new fangled vehicle (our automobile) in which he found himself travelling.

He would have regretted to find at the bottom of the steep hill on East Street a half mile from the tavern, where we cross the brook, that the old mill has been burned down and has not been rebuilt, but he should have been pleased to see that the oldest house in Litchfield was being restored. I doubt if he would have known how old it was, for it was standing in his great-grandfather's time, and his great-great-grandfather died in 1730. He would have probably been glad that if the old door didn't suit, and Mis' Richards had to hire one of these new-fangled architects to make her a new one, that she picked on young Mr. Woolsey, one of the old Yale family, you know. But the new door is so in keeping with the old house that he probably wouldn't have noticed the change.

Across the road he would have recognized Echo Farm with its tiny porch and Palladian window and would have felt no comment necessary; it looks just the same as it always did; and from Echo Farm to East Litchfield he would have found only one new house, although in the small plain

ECHO FARM, LITCHFIELD, CONNECTICUT
Built about 1737

Doorway and overhang

THE WHITMAN HOUSE,
FARMINGTON CONNECTICUT

Overhang embellished by "drop" ornament

farmsteads along the road he would have found Zuccas and Bodanskis working the fields which used to belong to Demmings and Fosters.

He might have wondered at the new concrete bridge and the railroad tracks at East Litchfield had we let him see them, but by our agreeable conversation, we would have diverted his mind until we had crossed the new state road up the Naugatuck Valley, and had turned up what looks like the yard of the corner farm house into the road to Harwinton; and as we climbed the long mile to the Tavern at the cross road to Torrington, he would have seen no change at all, for there is no house or relic of a house in that mile.

He (having come from 1823) would have wanted to stop for a little refreshment at the tavern, but it has long since been closed, and is now very rusty and down at heel; and then we would have driven another two miles along a narrow tree shaded soggy road until we came to what was in his day the newest house in Harwinton, the Wilson house on which the paint had but dried in 1833. The man who built the Wilson house wasn't any of your back woods builders! He knew a thing or two about this new Greek architecture Asher Benjamin had written a book about, and he got some of the best of it into this house, even if Mr. Wilson did insist on the recessed side porch so fashionable in Har-

CONGREGATIONAL
CHURCH,
FARMINGTON,
CONNECTICUT

*The Church at
Harwinton is almost
a literal copy of this one*

winton but on this porch he used what was called the "column in antis" motive with two story columns two feet in diameter. These so obstructed the porch that an irreverent generation has taken them out and stored them in the barn.

Harwinton would have seemed very familiar to our passenger, for while he would have noticed some "new" houses built around 1830 (in the biggest and best of which Henry Hornbostel lives) he would have been glad to see the old Academy behind the Messenger house, and would probably have regretted as we did that the cupola has been taken off and a tin roof substituted for the ancient shingles. But the Messenger house, once the home of the family of the first settlers in Harwinton, is in perfect condition, probably because it is owned by a gentleman who lives in what our passenger knew as Fort Duquesne.

The old fellow would have told us some interesting things about Harwinton; how it was settled in 1686 partly by people from Hartford, and partly by people from Windsor; and how those two towns quarrelled so over the new settlement that it finally set up for itself on the 11th of May in 1733, choosing as its name the combination Har-win-ton from Hart-ford-town, and Wind-sor-town. But he could have told us what his father had very likely *not* told him, of how many hogsheads of cider and barrels of rum were drunk when they "raised" the church.

If he had been told what we were doing he would have been sorry not to see us stop and photograph the church which is one of the most delightful of the old New England Meeting houses with a steeple, in what Mr. Hornbostel called the Chippendale style, which may be that too, for all I know, although it is almost a literal copy of another church on the Litchfield-Hartford road, the one at Farmington. The old Town Hall, which must have been new in his day has unfortunately been destroyed and replaced by a brick building which Mr. Hornbostel, the architect, has thoughtfully designed following the motive of the old one.

Doorway Detail
THE RICHARDS HOUSE,
LITCHFIELD, CONNECTICUT

THE RICHARDS HOUSE,
LITCHFIELD, CONNECTICUT

Built about 1730.
Restorations soon to be made

WILSON HOUSE,
HARWINTON,
CONNECTICUT
Built in 1833

OLD HARWINTON
ACADEMY, HARWITON,
CONNECTICUT
Built in 1783

DOORWAY AT HARWINTON, CONNECTICUT
Built in 1780

HOUSE AT HARWINTON CONNECTICUT
Built about 1810

But if he had inquired at any of the houses after the families of his old friends, and found them gone, he would probably not have been much surprised, for in 1820 there were only five families among the seventeen hundred and eighteen inhabitants, who had lived for twenty years in their original houses. These Harwinton people always were a restless lot.

By that time the old fellow would have been thirsty, missing his morning toddy at the Torrington Corner Inn, and without letting us stop at the Birge house or the Stone house, (so called because the lintels and sills are of stone, although the house itself was of brick with a wooden cornice and an entrancing old elliptical headed fan light and side light on the doorway) he would have hurried us up the hill to the old inn built in 1745 by one of the Abijah Catlins, and which was in my friend's

day the luncheon stop of the stages. In this plain little building five generations of Abijah Catlins kept tavern, and among the guests included General Washington and General Lafayette as well as many of the ancient Litchfield worthies. The stage route must have been much frequented, and the inn popular, for the second or third Abijah built himself a big comfortable house across the road from the inn, and spared no expense to make it the finest house in Harwinton, finer even than the Messenger house in the green. But our passenger has joined us a little too late, for only last year the last of Catlins sold the house to some foreigners from Torrington! The Catlin Homestead now owned by the Clevelands is really about as representative a piece of Connecticut architecture as one could wish for. It has all the motives which are distinctly of Connecticut origin, including a de-

THE MESSENGER HOUSE,
HARWINTON, CONNECTICUT
Built in 1783

DOORWAY OF THE
MESSENGER HOUSE

Built in 1783

lightful palladin window above the door and side-
lights like those in the Kingsberry house at Litchfield and the Cowls house at Farmington, although
the treatment of them is flatter, the pilasters taking the place of columns in the lower border and
even the balustrades being sawn boards instead of
turned. The side porch has the two story free
standing order within a recess, and in the
gable ends in the third story sort of baby palladin
window lights the attic. The house is unfortunately on the south side of the road and shadowed by
very heavy trees so that a successful photograph
of it is almost impossible. It really is one of the
most notable houses in New England and its pleasant owners appreciate this fact and are proposing
to restore it to its original condition both in de-

THE ABIJAH CATLIN
HOMESTEAD,
HARWINTON,
CONNECTICUT

*Built in 1795.
It has all the motives
which are distinctly
of Connecticut origin*

sign and furnishings, a thing which we do not always have the luck to find.

The five miles from Harwinton to Burlington would have shown our passenger nothing either old or new except a couple of pleasant old farmhouses, built about the time of his last trip; and we would have set him down in Burlington at the Brown Inn, facing the green with its small pa-

thetic monument to the town's dead in the World War. Around the green he would have seen old friends, and no intruders; but he would have sighed to see them so forlorn, the lovely porch of the Inn shorn of its columns, and the houses grimy and unkempt except for one smart little house at the head of the green where the road to Winsted forks from the old stage coach road.

FIRST
CONGREGATIONAL
CHURCH,
ON THE GREEN,
CANTERBURY,
CONNECTICUT

*Rebuilt in 1784, on the
site of former churches*

Old Canterbury, Connecticut

AMONG the score of early colonial hill towns in Windham County, Connecticut, Canterbury is probably the most interesting and appealing. Not only are there several buildings of unusual architectural merit, but, fortunately these have been preserved in their original state and unspoiled by "modern improvements." In addition to this, the whole village is harmonious, having happily escaped the march of progress and lying peacefully "off the map".

Located on a long irregular ridge, about 200 feet above the broad valley of the Quinnebaug River, this small village has only a dozen old houses near the Green, and another dozen scattered along the old "ways" leading north and south. The result is a town of remarkably intimate and alluring quality.

The calm is unbroken by railroad, trolley or jitney line. Neither does any State road nor motor "tour" pass through the town, with their consequent hot-dog stands, gasolene stations and giant bill-boards. There are no mills, millionaires or summer boarders to bring in money and inevitable changes. There is now but one small general store, and even the former Post Office has been removed to the railroad station, some four miles away. To visit this little town today is therefore quite like stepping back one hundred years.

The Township of Canterbury was the fourth settlement in the county. The Quinnebaug valley was first settled as early as 1680 by men from Norwich. Major Fitch and his family built the first permanent house in 1697, at what was then called "Peagscomsuck," the Indian name for what was later Canterbury. With hundreds of farms and thousands of acres at his disposal, Major Fitch selected for his permanent residence this land near the Quinnebaug River now the Township of Canterbury, surely a great compliment from one of his travelled experience.

The Town of Plainfield about three miles to the east was organized in 1699. The difficulty, however, of crossing the Quinnebaug River to attend religious worship was the chief ground for starting a separate town organization for Canterbury on the west bank of the River. In 1703, Town privileges were granted, and it was formally separated from Plainfield. There were only ten resi-

FIRST CONGREGATIONAL CHURCH, ON THE GREEN, CANTERBURY, CONNECTICUT

West Front
Built in 1784

Estabrook, and prepared to build their first Meeting House on the site of the Green. This church was established in 1711 with a membership of only twenty-five.

"Suitable ways" were laid out, connecting the town with Plainfield three miles east; Norwich, 15 miles south; Windham, 10 miles west and Woodstock, 20 miles north. These were the closest and only other settlements at this time. The chief difficulty, however, was in maintaining a bridge over the turbulent Quinnebaug. The two towns of Canterbury and Plainfield were put to constant trouble and expense in rebuilding the bridges as the severe ice flows in the early spring kept carrying them away.

Obadiah Johnson was allowed to keep a house for Public Entertainment "provided he keeps good order," and here town meetings were held and public business transacted. A schoolmaster was employed to "perambulate" the town, there being no school house at this time.

Major Fitch was the leading citizen and by far the most picturesque figure in the early days. He was a friend of education and endowed Yale College in 1701 with 600 acres of land. He was genial, generous and hospitable, but somewhat "over-convivial" in his habits; so that he was sometimes compelled to make confessions to the Church as well as to the State. His social position drew many people around him. His plantation was recognized as a place of consequence, the first and, for a long time, the only settlement between Norwich and Woodstock. One of the most prominent men in the whole state, his popularity gradually decreased owing to public jealousy excited by his immense land operations.

The period of greatest prosperity in the town

dents, but their "character and circumstances made amends for their small number." They were men of means and position, accustomed to the management of public affairs and well fitted to initiate and carry on the settlement of the new Township. But as all of the good land was held by these original ten settlers, there was no inducement for others to join, and the population increased but slowly.

They soon procured a minister, Rev. Samuel

FIRST
CONGREGATIONAL
CHURCH,
ON THE GREEN,
CANTERBURY,
CONNECTICUT

Detail of Main Doorway

THE TURNPIKE HOUSE,
CANTERBURY, CONNECTICUT

Detail of Doorway

came immediately after the Revolutionary War. Master Adam's School established on the Green in 1796 was an immediate success. The young blood of the town were energetic, and business and trade were active. Cultivated "solid" men gave prominence to the town. Few country towns could boast such social attractions. Dr. Harris, one of the most genial and hospitable of men, had

THE PRUDENCE
CRANDALL HOUSE,
ON THE GREEN,
CANTERBURY,
CONNECTICUT
Originally built by
Squire Elisha Payne

THE PRUDENCE CRANDALL HOUSE,
ON THE GREEN,
CANTERBURY, CONNECTICUT

Detail of Entrance Pavilion

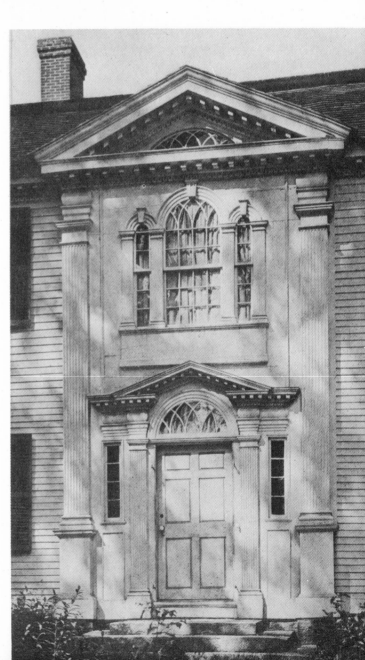

a new model house with a conservatory that was
the wonder of all the county.

Architecturally it was extremely fortunate that
the greatest prosperity of the town came at this
period of good taste. After the Civil War, the
prosperity declined, there being no special business interests to draw in new residents or keep
the young people in the town. Altho' the histor-
ian of that time laments the fall of the town from
"its former high estate", we cannot but rejoice
that it is preserved for us to see, just as it was a
century and a half ago.

The most striking piece of architecture in the
town is certainly the old Congregational Church,
rebuilt in 1784 on the site of former churches. It
has a most suitable and commanding position at

the top of the sharply sloping village green, surrounded by fine old maple trees. The recessed porch with its four square Doric columns is an unusual and most fitting solution of the entrance portico. The recess seems to give it a quiet religious quality not obtained by the usual projecting portico. It seems to invite one to enter in a spirit of quiet and privacy, and is worthy of most careful study. There are two small side doors from this porch for entrance, and one very broad central double doorway for exit and special occasions. The porch also, being completely protected on three sides, forms a very sheltered place in bad weather for the congregation to exchange friendly greetings before and after service. The floor is paved with very large granite slabs, and there are radiating granite steps outside the center bay. The side bays are protected by a very delicate and inconspicuous picket railing. The octagonal spire is less ornate than many, but entirely pleasing in its proportions. The uneven sides to the octagon and their different treatment are of special interest.

The private houses in the town are generally of quite a distinct type, and were probably all designed by an Architect named Dyer. The chief characteristic of this Canterbury type of house is the low-pitched dormer-less hip roof, with pediment ends to the deck roof, giving a "semi-monitor" effect. This treatment pleasantly increases the length of the ridge and gives a horizontal footing for the two chimneys. The result gives a comfortable, restful and convincing look to the whole composition.

Another feature of these houses is the two story pilaster which occurs not only at the corners, but framing the central pavilions on one and often two fronts. Another characteristic is the Palladian window over the front entrance, usually the side windows, as well as the central window having keyed arches. Still another feature is the very wide composition of the front entrance, with pilasters, fan light and side lights.

The characteristic most interesting to the architect, however, is the scale and individuality of the conventional late 18th Century Georgian details. These are usually a little too heavy for domestic purposes and uninteresting in their uniformity. In Canterbury, however, the scale of the details has been slightly reduced with a very just

West Front

THE CAPTAIN JOHN CLARK HOUSE, SOUTH CANTERBURY, CONNECTICUT

Built in 1732, enlarged about 1790

sense of fitness. Examples of the individual variation are seen in the reeding on the cornice and the Greek fret dentil course and panelled frieze.

The most famous of these old houses is the so-called Prudence Crandall house, originally built by Squire Elisha Payne on the Green. In 1831, Miss Crandall bought the house, left vacant by the Squire's death, and opened a fashionable young ladies' boarding school, much to the pride and satisfaction of the town. About a year later with the support of the leading Abolitionists in Boston, she suddenly changed it to a school for colored girls, much to the disgust and indignation of the aristocratic families. She was threatened with ejection, and even special State Legislation against Colored Schools was put through by her enemies. She was even kept a short while in the Brooklyn Jail. But the long drawn out trials brought no definite results, and these persecutions greatly strengthened her friends and supporters. Finally however, all the windows of the house were broken in one night by exasperated townsmen and she and her colored pupils were forced to leave the town. "Thus ended the generous and philanthropic Christian enterprise of Miss Prudence Crandall."

The Crandall house is not a large house. With a frontage of 44 feet it has a depth of only 32 feet. There are four rooms on each floor, separated by two chimneys. The front rooms, however, are

THE DAVID KINNE HOUSE, BLACK HILL, CANTERBURY, CONNECTICUT
Built in 1780, enlarged during 1815

THE CAPTAIN JOHN CLARK HOUSE,
SOUTH CANTERBURY, CONNECTICUT

Detail of the Main Cornice

THE CAPTAIN JOHN CLARK HOUSE,
SOUTH CANTERBURY, CONNECTICUT

Entrance Pavilion—West Front

Detail of Doorway

THE LA VALLE HOUSE, CANTERBURY, CONNECTICUT

about twice as large as the rear rooms. The stair hall goes back only half the depth of the house. The pediment end of the deck roof has an oval decorated with radiating incised lines. The whole oval was formerly painted dark to count as more of a feature than it does at present. The central pavilion facing the Green projects 8 inches in the front of the main line of the house, and is typical of the Canterbury type. Fluted pilasters on plain pedestals support the pediment. The second story Palladian window rests on a continuous pedestal —the absolute plainness of which is a pleasing contrast to the surrounding richness.

The next most important house is the Capt. John Clark house at the south end of the Town, built about 1732, and enlarged about 1790 by Capt. Clark, an eccentric Englishman with ample means and patriarchal family, who continued his eccentric and autocratic ways until the ripe age of 101. This Clark house is very spacious in every way, with a frontage of 46 feet and a depth of 42 feet. The four rooms on each floor are very large and the central hallway running through the entire house is 11 feet wide. The house has two fronts, both treated architecturally. The main front, facing the high road leading to Norwich, has free standing columns, which makes it even more elegant than the Crandall house. The south front, facing the maple lined driveway, has a Roman Doric order enclosing the arched fan, but with no side lights. Both fronts have very narrow clapboards, only 2½ inches to the weather, giving an air of great refinement.

The David Kinne house is to the east of the River, on the top of Black Hill, so called because it was frequently burned over by the Indians. Later, when William Kinne set out a double row of maples along the whole mile of the road leading up to his house, it was suggested that the name be changed to Green Hill. This house was built originally in 1780, with the front facing south. It was enlarged in 1815, the old kitchen at the rear forming a new central hall 12 feet wide opening on to the center of the new east front. It

THE DAVID KINNE HOUSE, BLACK HILL, CANTERBURY, CONNECTICUT

South Front Entrance

is interesting to note that these two fronts are now identical in treatment. The monitor roof is a direct result of influence from Rhode Island, only a few miles to the east.

Other houses of interest are located on or near the Green. In all there are only a hand-full. But, like the original citizens of the town, their qual-ity more than makes up for their small number. No unkept lawns, overgrown paths or wandering poultry can in any way lessen their aristocratic assurances. Their sophisticated refinement and good taste are intrinsic and lasting. May they re-main unspoiled and cherished for another cen-tury at least, a constant joy and inspiration!

Detail of Portico
THE PERKINS HOUSE, WINDHAM, CONNECTICUT
Built in 1832

Hill Towns
Of Windham County,
Connecticut

THE early settlers in the northeast corner of Connecticut—Windham County—located their towns on the hill-tops to secure greater safety from the Indians. They planned more wisely than they knew; for not only were their towns preserved from destruction by the Indians in the late 17th Century, but also from destruction by industrialism and Victorian prosperity in the late 19th Century.

The first period in the history of these towns was a tale, many times retold, of hardship, struggle and endurance. The region was known as early as 1635, as it was on the direct route from the Massachusetts Bay Colony to the Connecticut River Settlements. This "hideous and trackless wilderness" was traversed by only the roughest sort of trail, known as the "Connecticut Path". The first definite settlement of any kind within the county area was made in 1686, by thirty courageous families from Roxbury, Massachusetts, who toiled along the eighty miles of wild country to form a new community at "New Roxbury", which later became known as Woodstock. Settlers in other parts of the county came from Norwich, Connecticut, which lay several miles to the south of the present County line. All had the same trying experiences. Land purchases from the Indians were most uncertain. The English Governor of the Connecticut Colony added to this uncertainty by trying to appropriate all these purchases to the Crown, saying that the signature of an Indian was not worth more than

a scratch of a bear's paw. The French and Indian War still further delayed settlements everywhere. Then came the clearing of the ground, building the houses and barns, disputes about boundaries and the difficult task of establishing a minister and raising a church in each remote settlement. However, before 1775 all this was fairly accomplished almost everywhere in the county.

The second period, after the Revolution, was one of great prosperity throughout the county. Stage-coach roads were built up to these towns, no matter how steep or high or rough the hill. They were no longer isolated and remote. They were connected by high roads to Hartford, Providence, Norwich and the towns in Massachusetts. Stage-coach inns were opened and flourished in each town. Three of these inns are now open and still offer their hospitality all the year around; the Ben Grosvenor Inn at Pomfret, the Chelsea Inn at Hampton Hill and the Windham Inn at Windham. Their decorative old sign boards are still swinging in the breeze.

The third period came with the railroads and the building of factories in the last half of the 19th Century. The railroad naturally followed the rivers and valleys and several modern manufacturing towns sprang up along the Natchaug and Quinebaug Rivers. The old stage-coach lines were discontinued and the commerce with the outside world lapsed; so that the old hill towns again found themselves left high and dry. But, though this may have been a disappointment to a few ambitious merchants in these towns, it proved to be a blessing in disguise. Well removed from the nearest railroad, they are preserved today as delightful residential villages, with all the charm and atmosphere of a hundred years ago.

Canterbury is the most appealing of the sixteen old towns in Windham County.

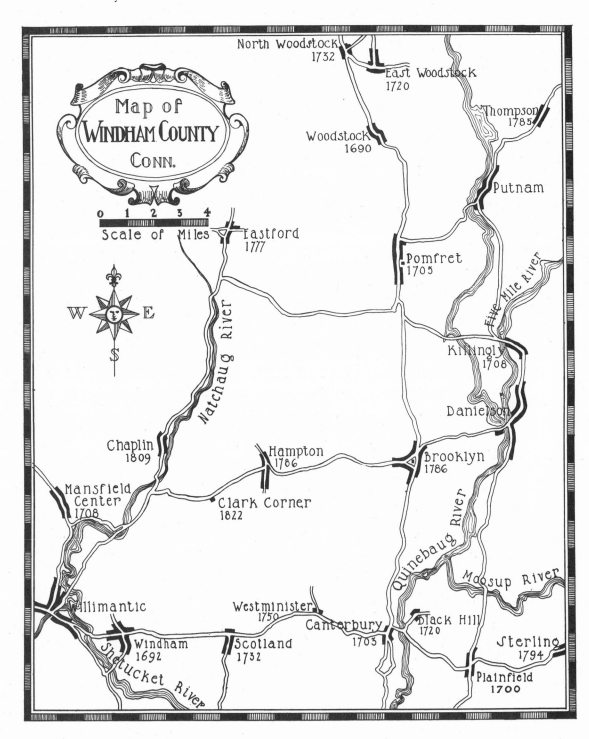

Map of
WINDHAM COUNTY
CONN.

0 1 2 3 4
Scale of Miles

W E S

North Woodstock 1732
East Woodstock 1720
Thompson 1785
Woodstock 1690
Putnam
Eastford 1777
Pomfret 1705
Five Mile River
Natchaug River
Killingly 1708
Danielson
Chaplin 1809
Hampton 1786
Brooklyn 1786
Mansfield Center 1708
Clark Corner 1822
Quinebaug River
Moosup River
Willimantic
Westminister 1750
Canterbury 1703
Black Hill 1720
Sterling 1794
Windham 1692
Scotland 1732
Plainfield 1700
Shetucket River

WINDHAM was settled in 1689 by sixteen gentlemen from Norwich. Its unusual advantages and proximity to Norwich attracted a superior class of citizens, men of character, position and public spirit. Windham Green soon increased in business and importance. Here were town clerk, constable, justices and leading men. There was much good fellowship among early settlers, feasting, merry-making and interchange of hospitalities. The young people remained at home, marry-

By 1750 social life was noted as exceedingly "hilarious and enjoyable"; "jaunting and junketing" were popular. Windham people were especially noted for their love of fun and frolic, bantering and jesting others. One joke was turned on them, however. Fear of the French and the Indians was still persisting, when on a very dark, sultry summer night, a roar and tumult filled the town. The people, perplexed and greatly frightened, stayed behind barred doors and listened

THE WEBB HOUSE, WINDHAM, CONNECTICUT

ing mostly among their own townspeople, till, in the process of years, the whole population was knit together in one great family circle. In 1726 Windham was made shire town of the county. Though far to the southwest of the centre of the county, no one thought of disputing her claim. She had far outstripped her sister townships in population, wealth, cultivation and political influence. The first court of the County was held at Windham Green and soon after a court-house and jail were erected.

with horror, no one venturing out to face the foe. Next morning it was discovered that it was only a migration through the town of noisy bull-frogs in search of water, their own pond having dried up. Much to the mortification of the Windham people, the story flew all over the county and the country.

Just south of the Green stands the old Webb House, which was built during the early days of Windham's settlement. The house has an unusual L-shaped plan, with two long fronts of equal architecture which flourished in the United States during the period of the Classic Revival. The house as well as the portico has a broad pediment. The front is faced with tongued and grooved siding put on vertically, giving a flat serene background and forming a pleasing contrast to the fluted columns of the front portico. There are two chimneys on each end with the side walls between them covered with clapboards. The wing at the side is also clapboarded. The Ionic portico (frontispiece) is so consummately well proportioned that we are not surprised to find that the designer gave special study to the most advantageous manner of spacing the columns, to further the design as a whole. It will be seen by studying the front elevation that the central span is distinctly broader than the bays on each side of it, in order not to hide or "crowd" the unusually broad front doorway with its Doric columns "in antis" and side lights. This uneven spacing of the columns also gives an hospitable effect to the centre entrance, stability to the corners and a delightful rhythm to the whole portico.

Side Door
THE WEBB HOUSE, WINDHAM, CONN.

length; one facing the main road and the other a side lane. There is a high Doric porch on the street front, reached by a long flight of steps which run parallel with the wall. A delicate diamond design railing is a feature of the porch. There is a wide front doorway with fluted pilasters and double doors of five panels each. The top panels are rounded. On the other façade there is a simple and very flat doorway, not, however, without architectural interest. A pleasing effect of substance and dignity is obtained by the unusually broad treatment of the frame. A moulded architrave of the usual width is separated from the door opening by a plain band seven inches wide and from the narrow clapboards by another plain band, making the total width of the frame eighteen inches. A deep flat arch of solid wood, carved to simulate stone quoins, springs from the outside corners of the frame. The flat arch feature is repeated over all the first floor windows.

The Perkins House, illustrated on the opposite page, was not built until 1832, but it is surely one of the very best examples of the type of domestic

East Porch
THE WEBB HOUSE, WINDHAM, CONN.

THE PERKINS HOUSE, WINDHAM, CONNECTICUT
Built in 1832

"SQUIRE BOSWORTH'S CASTLE", EASTFORD, CONN.

POMFRET AND VICINITY: Pomfret owes its origin to the courage of one Captain John Blackwell, an English Puritan, who had fled to America at the restoration of the Stuarts in 1687. He was in Woodstock in its time of peril and panic, caused by the Indian Wars, and rendered valuable service by going out on the "frontier" to what is now Pomfret and "standing his ground" against the enemy.

Mrs. John Grosvenor was among the settlers that straggled into Pomfret after the end of the Indian Wars in 1696. Her portion was the fairest

creetly kept in the rear, so that the long line of the quaint two-story portico still graces the street as it did a hundred and fifty years ago. This shallow portico is only six feet wide, with a flat wood ceiling painted lavender blue. The posts are eighteen feet high but only eight inches square at the bottom, tapering to seven inches at the top.

Another two-story portico is found at the Colonel Lyons House at East Woodstock, a few miles north of Pomfret. Four slender and graceful Doric columns support a low pediment roof. A shallow balcony with a picket railing is sus-

THE BEN GROSVENOR INN, POMFRET, CONNECTICUT

part of the township, the upper part of the present village. Her grandson, Ebenezer Grosvenor, was the noted landlord of the Pomfret Tavern, a resort much frequented in the stirring times just before 1776 when rum and debate flowed with equal freedom.

Prosperous summer residents have modernized and enlarged almost all the simple old 18th Century houses that once lined Pomfret Street. None are left in their original state except the old Ben Grosvenor Inn, (shown on this page). Even this has modern additions, but these have been dis-

pended at the second floor level. The running diamond decoration below the cornice adds to the delicate refinement.

The most surprising and unusual house in the neighborhood is certainly "Squire Bosworth's Castle", at Eastford. Perched on a very high, steep hill above the town, the vertical effect is still further enhanced by a two-story monitor roof, containing a lodge room with a fireplace at each end. The interior is literally carved within an inch of its life, with fine scale and highly original motifs worthy of careful inspection.

THE COL. LYONS HOUSE, EAST WOODSTOCK, CONN.

THE SNOW HOUSE, CHAPLIN, CONNECTICUT
Built in 1822

Detail of Entrance   *Detail of Cupola*

THE OLD TOWN HALL, BROOKLYN, CONNECTICUT

CHAPLIN is the latest of the old towns to be founded, but by no means the least interesting. Its first permanent settler was Deacon Benjamin Chaplin, who, in 1740, went from Pomfret out into the "wilderness"—some ten miles to the southwest—took land on the Natchaug River and cleared himself a homestead. In 1747 he married the Widow Mary Ross and built a large and handsome mansion. It still stands, a monument to his success and known yet as the Old Chaplin House. Deacon Chaplin, a man of marked character, shrewd and far-sighted, foresaw the growth of the community that was to bear his name, and bought up much land at low figures, laid out farms, built houses and barns and ruled as the lord of the manor. Just why no church was built at the same time we do not know. Certain it is that Deacon Chaplin was a man of religious convictions, for, with a daughter on a pillion behind

him to jump down to open intervening bars and gates, he was accustomed to ride six miles to attend church at South Mansfield. At his death, in 1795, he left a generous fund to found a church near his home "before January 1, 1812". Accordingly, a religious society, called after the Deacon, was founded by the farmers living in the neighborhood. But, due to various delays and disagreements, the church was not actually finished until 1820.

The present town of Chaplin extends along a main street, laid parallel with the river. The church is situated about midway of the street, on a slight rise of ground. Although the church itself is of no great architectural interest or merit, there are at least a dozen neighboring houses, rich in fine detail, that are very good examples of the 1820 period.

On each side of the church are twin houses,

THE "PENNY" LINCOLN HOUSE, SCOTLAND, CONNECTICUT
Built in 1835

very similar to a third, the Hope House, at the north end of the town. All three are the two-chimney houses so frequently found in Windham County, with a pediment having a pitch of 30 degrees, enclosing a decorative fan window. The Hope House, the most interesting of the three

THERE are other 18th Century farmhouses in Windham County, scattered sparsely beyond the village greens. They are plainer and perhaps less interesting architecturally than the more prosperous and decorated houses in the towns. There is, however, a definite type found in this county that is exemplified by the "Penny" Lincoln House at Scotland, illustrated above. This two-chimney type is as characteristic of Northeastern Connecticut as the one-central-chimney type is typical of Central and Western Connecticut. The plan consists of four rooms (each about 12 ft. x 18 ft.), two on each side of a

central hall, and separated by the large chimneys and deep flanking closets. One of the outer closets is often used as a vestibule to the side door. There are overhanging gable ends, but no overhangs elsewhere. There are five windows across the fronts, which are approximately forty feet in length, but only two windows across the ends, which are approximately thirty feet deep, giving a pleasing contrast of much glass in front and much clapboarding at the ends. Altogether, this type is a stirring example of taste and good proportions, unadorned and needing no adornment.

Whether one prefers the simpler or the more decorated type of house, or one is more sympathetic to the 18th Century or early 19th Century type, there are many examples throughout this corner county of Connecticut which remain unspoiled and which are of real architectural interest and appeal.

ENTRANCE DOORWAY—OBADIAH ALCORN HOUSE, FARMINGTON, CONNECTICUT

Farmington, Connecticut

ARMINGTON! why did my thoughts constantly revert to Farmington, what was there to cause such a persistent subconscious recalling of the place? Here I was, thousands of miles away from that village, in a beautiful old town of France—Chartres, in fact, and all day long I had worked on procuring measured drawings of its lovely bits of detail, sketching its architecture and absorbing its past history, wandering through its cathedral and gazing upon its pulpit. By George! that's it, the pulpit, how it all came back to me now, as I lay stretched out upon my bed in a low ceilinged room of the Inn where I was sojourning after a full day of joy and of inspiring study, and now dead tired.

I understood clearly now; Chartres, with its centuries old history, its traditions, its beauty and its architecture brought home vividly our own lack of something to show and leave to the world. I could not help thinking of how ridiculous it would be to travel the distance I had, and to register at an hotel in Passaic, New Jersey, or Nyack, New York, or Lansing, Michigan, in order that I might study our own architecture and make measured drawings of its mouldings and become enthralled by it all.

Then my mind reverted again to Farmington and the few years I lived there, and really after all, there were places one could kick up an interest in, but how few and how meagre and small the number of examples in such communities. Still there was Farmington, it had probably more to show than the average.

Oh yes, that's it, that pulpit in the old church, I must be drowsy after my day, in fact I must have fallen asleep, for I was sitting stiff backed in one of the pews of the old church, the church upon completion of which the builder was paid partly by a hogshead of rum. Shades of Volstead, think of it, yes sir, it was the old minister delivering his sermon, pounding now upon the rail of that pulpit with its beautiful old Colonial detail; through the circular headed window the warm spring sun streamed into the church, the windows were open and one could hear the song of happy young birds. Old Abigail Potter made that pulpit, and what a wonderful bit of work it was, he loved it, was proud of it, and had enjoyed the work of doing it. I must stand up, the old minister is through, wonder what he said? That pulpit certainly diverted my mind from the sermon. Oh there, going out now, what a delightful day, there is old Captain Gibbons, he is working on that new canal that is going to connect Farmington with New Haven. Must

117

be discussing it with his friends. He lives in the house on Farmington Avenue. Oh yes, he's just had an old knocker made of brass and lettered with his name for the front door, he needs it too, I spent many moments trying to make him hear my knock on the door, getting sore knuckles for my efforts.

Guess I must start meandering down the road a bit, been invited to dinner at the Cowles'. My how Abigail loves to surprise us, just look at that door to the Deming house, has pilaster caps, all of his own conception, but what a lovely solid panelled door, hope no one ever destroys it, the whole door is rather exceptional, but then doorways are so alluring to work on. Just look at that one of Gay's, the panelling almost like the Demmings', but entirely different, and then the door on Obadiah Alcorn's without a cap, what a lovely fence too. The cornice also is interesting, remember how they struggled over the bracket at the corner, don't think there is another like it.

Up through the trees on the upper street, I see the old Whitman house with that overhanging second floor; we have only an Indian here and there now, but a few years back they used to shoot Indians through a hole from the second floor in that overhang, but I must be

SIDE PORCH OF THE GENERAL COWLES HOUSE, FARMINGTON, CONNECTICUT

getting along, the old town is full of those bits of Colonial details, cornices, doorways, rain-water heads, and I must make some sketches here some day. There is the house of General Cowles with two curious features, the front door with its inverted columns and the side porch with its five columns and pediment. How that centre column seems to hold up the Palladian window in the pediment, and what a thin amount of masonry over those arches at the porch floor level. Still, the whole thing looks well, and quite like Charleston. It's a stranger in our Northern village, but very welcome.

And now I am at the gate of Admiral Cowles' residence where I am to dine. No gate quite like this one, you know, the house was the product of a young English Army officer while stationed over here during the Revolution, who must have been an architect in England, drafted into the service. He left his imprint by way of

ENTRANCE GATEWAY—THE ADMIRAL COWLES HOUSE, FARMINGTON, CONNECTICUT

THE ADMIRAL COWLES HOUSE,
FARMINGTON, CONNECTICUT

BRACKET AND DROP DETAIL
THE "OLDER" COWLES HOUSE,
FARMINGTON, CONNECTICUT

[*Built about* 1661]

the Cowles' house; he must have been in India too, see the swastika worked into the gate. I knock at the front door and am admitted, it's a lovely bit of atmosphere that greets me; how hungry I am, and how I shall enjoy eating in such surroundings. Food tastes so different, doesn't it, in a pure white Colonial room with panelled walls and beautiful doors, and a lovely detailed cornice? Yes sir, that was a meal, and I am about to depart, the front door is open, and that gate through the front door, is it not a picture?

Well, as I step toward this sunlight, the picture begins to fade, I feel a sense of impending danger, things begin to look dark, I am hungry, ah, I know, I was dreaming. I am in France at Chartres, but, I am also still hungry, hungry for a return of our delightful old village, thousands of miles is a long way to travel for inspiration; it ought to be near at home. Well there are a few villages offering their wealth, and of these few still left, one is Farmington.

THE PORTER HOUSE, FARMINGTON, CONNECTICUT

THE WHITMAN HOUSE,
FARMINGTON, CONNECTICUT

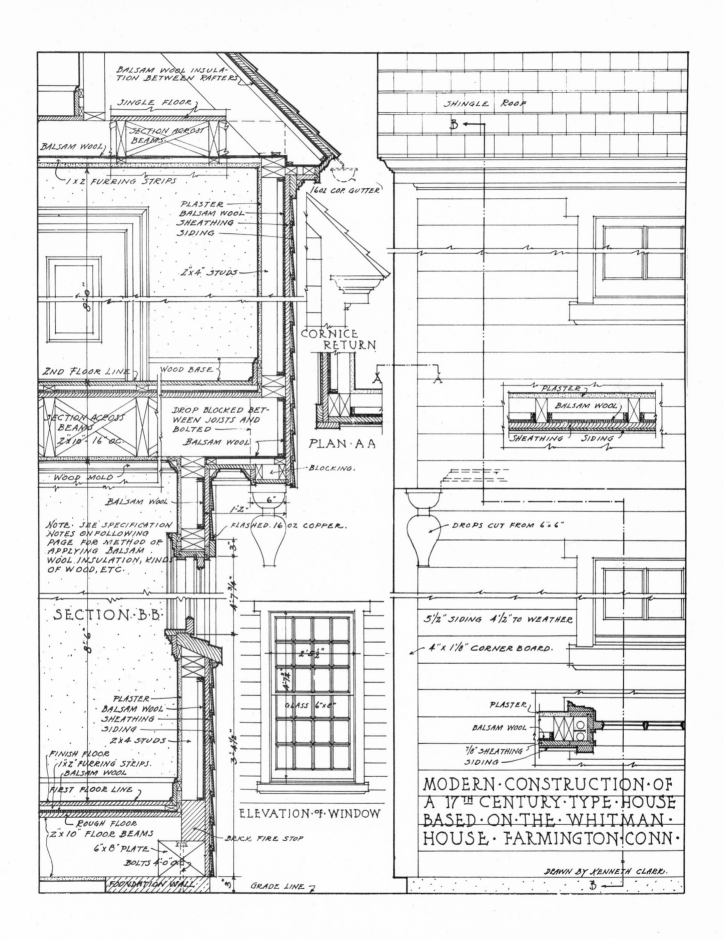

BALSAM WOOL INSULA-
TION BETWEEN RAFTERS

SINGLE FLOOR

SHINGLE ROOF

SECTION ACROSS
BEAMS.

BALSAM WOOL

B

1×2 FURRING STRIPS

PLASTER
BALSAM WOOL
SHEATHING
SIDING

1602 COP. GUTTER

2"×4" STUDS

CORNICE
RETURN

PLASTER
BALSAM WOOL

A

SHEATHING   SIDING

A

2ND FLOOR LINE   WOOD BASE

SECTION ACROSS
BEAMS
2"×10"-16"OC

DROP BLOCKED BET-
WEEN JOISTS AND
BOLTED

BALSAM WOOL

PLAN·AA

WOOD MOLD

BLOCKING.

NOTE· SEE SPECIFICATION
NOTES ON FOLLOWING
PAGE FOR METHOD OF
APPLYING BALSAM·
WOOL INSULATION, KINDS
OF WOOD, ETC.

BALSAM WOOL

DROPS CUT FROM 6"×6"

6"

1'-2"

FLASHED·16 OZ COPPER.

3"

SECTION·B·B

4'-7¾"

5½" SIDING 4½" TO WEATHER

4"× 1⅛" CORNER BOARD.

2'-4½"

PLASTER
BALSAM WOOL
SHEATHING
SIDING
2"×4" STUDS

4'-7¾"

GLASS 6"×6"

3'-4½"

PLASTER

BALSAM WOOL

FINISH FLOOR
1"×2" FURRING STRIPS.
BALSAM WOOL

FIRST FLOOR LINE

⅞" SHEATHING
SIDING

ROUGH FLOOR
2"×10" FLOOR BEAMS
6"×8" PLATE
BOLTS 4'-0" O.C.

BRICK FIRE STOP

MODERN·CONSTRUCTION·OF
A 17TH CENTURY·TYPE·HOUSE
BASED·ON·THE·WHITMAN·
HOUSE·FARMINGTON·CONN·

ELEVATION·OF·WINDOW

DRAWN BY KENNETH CLARK.

FOUNDATION WALL   GRADE LINE   B

125

MANTELPIECE SIDE OF THE WEST PARLOR

THE COWLES·LEWIS HOUSE

MEASURED DRAWINGS *from*
The George F. Lindsay Collection

LOOKING INTO THE DINING ROOM

BEDROOM MANTEL

HALL DOORWAY
THE COWLES-LEWIS HOUSE, FARMINGTON, CONNECTICUT

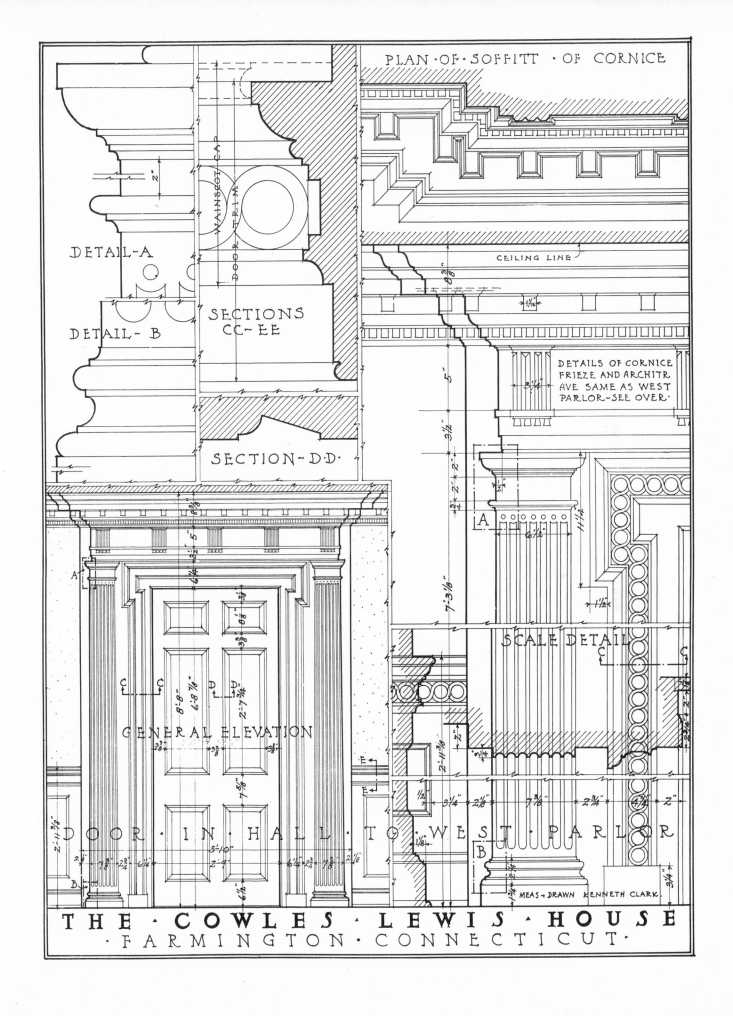

DETAIL-A

DETAIL-B

SECTIONS
CC ~ EE

WAINSCOT CAP

DOOR TRIM

SECTION-D·D

PLAN·OF·SOFFITT·OF CORNICE

CEILING LINE

DETAILS OF CORNICE
FRIEZE AND ARCHITR
AVE SAME AS WEST
PARLOR-SEE OVER

GENERAL ELEVATION

SCALE DETAIL

DOOR·IN·HALL·TO·WEST·PARLOR

MEAS + DRAWN   KENNETH CLARK

THE·COWLES·LEWIS·HOUSE
·FARMINGTON·CONNECTICUT·

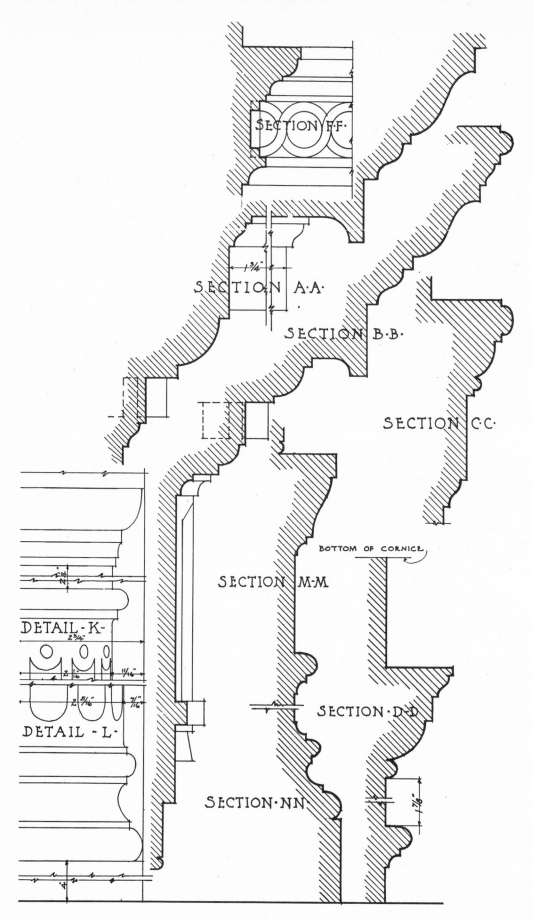

SECTION FF·

SECTION A·A·

SECTION B·B·

1¾"

SECTION C·C·

BOTTOM OF CORNICE

SECTION M·M

DETAIL · K ·

2¾"

2 1/16"   11/16"

DETAIL · L ·

2 5/16"   7/16"

SECTION · D·D·

SECTION · NN ·

7/8"

THE · COWLES

· FARMINGTON · CONNECTICUT ·

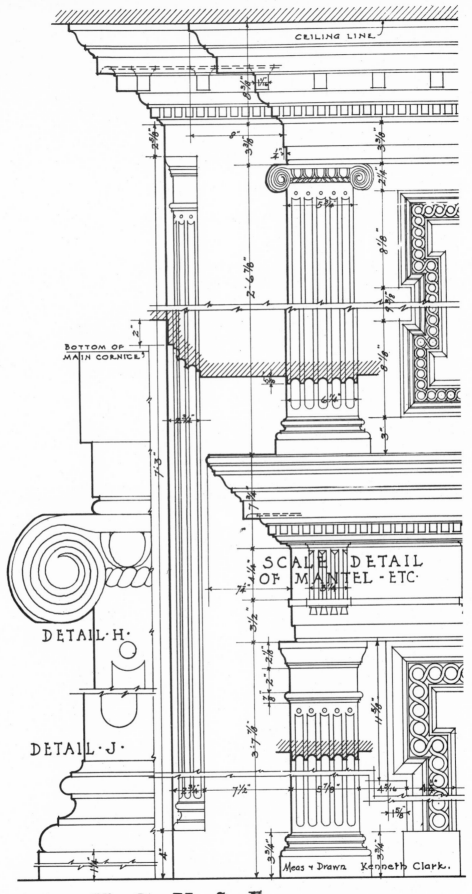

CEILING LINE

BOTTOM OF
MAIN CORNICE

SCALE DETAIL
OF MANTEL · ETC·

DETAIL·H·

DETAIL·J·

Meas & Drawn   Kenneth Clark.

L E W I S · H O U S E
· M A N T E L · W A L L · W E S T · P A R L O R ·

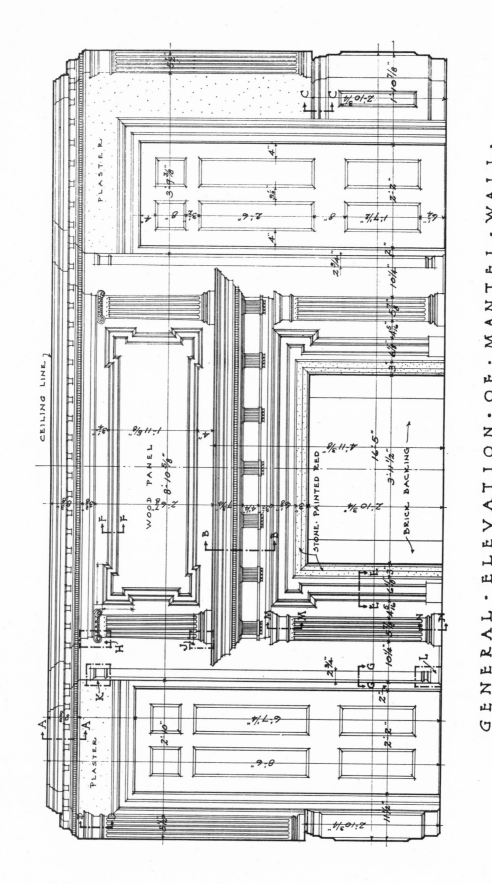

GENERAL·ELEVATION·OF·MANTEL·WALL·
SCALE ½" = 1'·0"

ALL MOLDING SECTIONS AND DETAILS·H·J·K·L·ARE SHOWN AT ½ FULL SIZE
OTHER PARTS AT SCALES MARKED.

DOORWAY DETAIL
THE GENERAL COWLES HOUSE, FARMINGTON, CONNECTICUT

THE MILLER HOUSE, DEERFIELD, MASSACHUSETTS.
Built *circa* 1710.

Old Deerfield, Massachusetts

I HOPE I shall be excused for mentioning the following bit of gossip which may seem to you to be but slightly connected with the strictest interpretation of my duty (for the present moment) as the introducer of the town of Deerfield, Massachusetts.

There was once a dignified old gentleman, who, like that other old gentleman in *"Cranford,"* was noted all through a certain provincial town for always saying *just* the proper thing at the proper time. Imagine, therefore, the horror of his friends, and especially of his wife, when in the course of talk one evening, it having been discovered that a certain young man in the company was a bachelor, the old gentleman, turning to him in a most cordial and enthusiastic way, said, "God bless you, sir; you are indeed a fortunate man, and—" "What!" said his horrified wife. "How can you say such a thing, sir? How CAN YOU?" "You interrupt me, ma'am," was the old gentleman's reply. "What I was saying was, that he is a very fortunate man, because he has great happiness to look forward to."

The only excuse that I can give you for having mentioned this at all is that it gives me some slight precedent for suggesting to you that if you have not been to Deerfield you also are a fortunate man in that you still have to experience the great pleasure of your first trip through the "pleasant streets of that dear old town."

Starting at one end of Deerfield's main street, following it to its opposite end, and continuing then to the outlying districts, you will pass few houses that are not of interest either because of some historical association or for the unusual merit of their architectural design.

For all practical purposes each Colonial town in New England repeats to a large degree in its general outlines the salient characteristics of every other Colonial town. And with the exception of some few idiosyncrasies common to certain localities (as the difference between Massachusetts and Rhode Island house planning), the individuality that distinguishes Salem under the influence of McIntire or Greenfield during the era of Asher Benjamin, does not appear until the very end of the eighteenth or the beginning of the nineteenth century.

In Deerfield no predominating style exists to the extent that it does, for instance, in Salem. The buildings, all of which are good examples of their particular time, extend over the whole possible range of periods from the earliest Jacobean-like work through the Asher Benjamin phase to (it must unfortunately be acknowledged in one instance) the days when "Egyptian-Moorish" and in another instance Preraphaelite Gothic were the proper thing in the vocabulary of the "genteel and up-to-date."

Of the hundred-odd houses in the town, the majority are of such great interest that this comparatively small philistine element will be wholly negligible in your enjoyment of this—as some of the natives boast—"sleepiest of all New England towns."

Exteriorly, as might be expected, the earliest houses here, as elsewhere, have little to show (excepting to the most enthusiastic of archæological experts) that is of interest as architectural detail.

The interest in the earliest houses lies for the most part in their splendid outline and in the carefully studied proportioning of window and door opening to the solid mass of plain

wall surfaces. And, as a rule, the detail which is found in connection with very early houses, when there is such detail as possesses distinctly architectural character, is an addition of later date than the building itself.

But whether this apparent sense of proportion was instinctive or purely accidental and governed, as may well have been the case, by structural exigencies into which no element of selection or proportioning was introduced by the builder, the result is none the less interesting and worthy of painstaking study by the architect of the present.

It is one of those facts which, like election-time orators, "need no preliminary introduction here," that Colonial architecture possesses little or no monumentality, and its chief power must be said to lie in its characteristic grouping and the ornamental treatments of certain single details of building. It was only in the Middle Period, starting at perhaps the 1740's or 1750's in New England, that a definitely architectural manner began to assert itself in interior and exterior finish and design.

Perhaps the most interesting earlier example of this later manner in Deerfield is found in the Old Manse, though competitors as to point of age are found in the Williams, Wetherald, and other houses.

The Williams house offers a number of problems, over the solution of which the inveterate expert might spend a large amount of time. As it stands to-day, the house may either be one built in 1707 to replace an earlier house which was erected by the town for Parson Williams and was burned in 1704, or it is possible that the 1707 house was destroyed and the present one erected in 1756 by the parson's son. Judged in the light of its condition as it stands to-day, one would not hesitate, in spite of all local traditions, to assign to it the later date.

The plan, for instance, very emphatically contradicts the assumption of its early erection.

A house in Massachusetts built in 1707 would, of course, have had a central chimney stack, with the rooms and entry grouped around it. The central chimney, however, does not appear in the house at the present time, and the fireplaces are at the central axis of the rear wall of the front rooms on each side of the hall.

THE ROOT HOUSE, DEERFIELD, MASSACHUSETTS. FRONT DOOR DETAIL.

THE FRARY HOUSE, DEERFIELD, MASSACHUSETTS.

Part of the building was erected in 1683 and is the oldest house in the town.

FRONT DOOR DETAIL.
THE SMITH HOUSE.
DEERFIELD, MASSACHUSETTS.

The entrance door and frame, the window frames and the interior panelling and staircase also suggest the work of the middle rather than the early years of the century.

In spite of all this, however, the solution seems to be that here, as in other authenticated instances in the town, the house was changed and such additions made from time to time as were suggested and made possible by the prosperity of successive owners. Instances are not unknown in Deerfield in which the central chimney was removed at an early date and the plan and interior and exterior details so rearranged as to suggest a middle eighteenth-century erection.

Undoubtedly as it stands to-day, the Williams house consists of the original 1707 frame with improvements in plan and ornamental detail in the taste of the year 1756. It is known that at that date the parson's son, Elijah, "made certain marked alterations in the house, both external and internal," and probably left the building in substantially its present condition.

Richard B. Derby, in his "Early Houses of the Connecticut River Valley" (in which, by the way, he has deprived the present number of some of its best thunder by anticipating it in the publication of the charming Asher Benjamin-like Horatio Hoyt house, and others), suggests in the instance of the doorway of the Williams house, and the same thing would hold good for the window frames, a date "probably several decades later" than 1756.

THE BISHOP PORTER HOUSE, DEERFIELD, MASS.
FRONT DOOR DETAIL.
Built in 1803.

Whatever may be its date, the house is certainly of unusual interest. The scheme of fenestration and the broad blank space between the door and windows on the first floor, and the compact spacing of the windows themselves, are noteworthy features which must be taken into consideration in solving the problem of the remarkable appearance of solidity which the house presents.

The Miller house, built in 1710, which has three windows across the front on the second floor and two on the side (an unusual feature in early houses), might also be found after careful examination to be, in its present condition, the result of several additions. The house was built to replace an earlier one which was destroyed during the French and Indian War.

It will be remembered that Asher Benjamin lived and did some of his best work in Greenfield, a few miles distant from Deerfield. Undoubtedly careful investigation would uncover some hitherto unrecorded work by him in Deerfield. The doorway of the Bishop Porter house, a building that was erected in 1803, is most suggestive of his manner of design and is without doubt one of the most charming things of its sort in New England, as is also the doorway of the Hawkes house—which doorway has been used several times as a prototype, most successfully perhaps in connection with the restoration of a house dating from the Revolutionary period at Westport, Connecticut.

THE OLD MANSE, DEERFIELD, MASSACHUSETTS. Front Door Detail.

*An unusually complete example of the type. It still retains
the original door, boot scrapers and knocker. Built in 1768.*

THE OLD MANSE, DEERFIELD, MASSACHUSETTS.

A typical example of the work of the Middle—and historically Colonial—type, built in 1768.

There are earlier doorways, of course, and later ones, and earlier and later houses, and many local traditions and histories relating both to the houses and the people who lived in them, any one of which could be discussed at great length.

Taken all in all, Deerfield cannot be said to have any outstanding features of great monumentality, but it shows as clearly as perhaps any town of even larger size and greater importance could do, the complete evolution of architectural design from the earliest Colonial period to the later and more self-conscious design of the early nineteenth century.

Examples of the earliest period are lacking, excepting for a few fragments of the so-called Indian House, dating from considerably before the Indian War, which are preserved by the local Historical Society in its museum. There are examples of each of the successive developments

which came with the later periods, and some of these examples, as the illustrations will show, are of more than usual interest, and many of them, as, for instance, the Old Manse House, are of considerable importance. Those parts of the Indian House which are preserved, namely, an interesting batten doorway, and two brackets which were originally over the over-hang, and an interesting corner cupboard, are of unusual consequence. The contour of these brackets is particularly good.

It is easy to understand how tenaciously the builders of the earliest houses would have clung to the traditions of building that were common in the parts of England in which they had received their earliest training. It is interesting to follow the changes which took place as time went on in the design of the buildings. As these builders dropped out, the work was carried out by their apprentices and by the apprentices of

THE WETHERALD HOUSE, DEERFIELD, MASSACHUSETTS.   Built in 1752.

A less elaborate example than the Williams house of the earliest "architectural" type. Just the sort of house that witches might choose for disturbances, via the chimney route, but for the lamentable fact that the chimney has been torn out, giving the house thereby a decidedly bald and unfinished appearance.

**SIDE DOOR DETAIL.
THE HAWKES HOUSE,
DEERFIELD, MASSACHUSETTS.**
Built *circa* 1743.

these apprentices. There are also examples that show the tendency, as time went on and the settlers became more prosperous, to adopt the styles and manners of living that were found at that time in England. This change, however, does not show the work that was indigenous to the localities from which the builders came, but reflects, as nearly as changed conditions would allow, the latest style in design, and, for that matter, in every other detail of living.

During and shortly after the Revolution a new influence was introduced by the publication in America of reprints of English books on architecture, and at a later period by the books of Asher Benjamin.

Regarding the translation of a manner of building which is essentially one of brick and stone into the easily obtainable white pine and other local woods, Joy Wheeler Dow has this to say in his "American Renaissance":

"The predominant local color which distinguishes American Renaissance has been given to it by what has been our great national building commodity, *i.e.*, wood. The Greeks and Romans built of stone when they had the money to pay for it. Both stone and wood have grain, and have to be used with the same careful regard for it. Whether we build our columns up of stone or wooden sections—latitudinal in the one case, longitudinal in the other—to support a cornice also constructed in sections according to the convenient sizes of commerce for the particular material, makes no difference to the canons of art so long as we are not trying to deceive or to imitate one material with another simply with that end in

view. It is extremely doubtful if our American ancestors were ever guilty of premeditated deception. Their material was an honest material, it had to be fashioned in some way; why not after the manner of the Renaissance?"

Sir Christopher Wren being the supreme actor upon the architectural stage in England at that time, it is natural that his influence would be strongly felt in the transplantation of architectural ideas between the two countries.

The earliest examples of Renaissance in Deerfield were not always accurate renderings of classic traditions in their design or construction, but there is a certain sturdiness and self-reliance shown in this work which speaks well for the mentalities of the men who were responsible for the work. The translation of details, which were primarily adopted for construction in stone, being built of wood, was carried out more often than not with an apparently large amount of skill, that after all makes the thing seem all right.

THE STEBBINS HOUSE, DEERFIELD, MASSACHUSETTS.
SIDE DOOR DETAIL.
Though less elaborate than the front door
it shows remarkable consistence in design.

Attention cannot be called too often to the fact that American work does not show a real independence in design until the early years of the nineteenth century. Such men as MacIntire, Hoadley, McComb and others not only contributed very largely to the development of architectural design in America; theirs was a very definite and valuable contribution to the total of the architectural history of the nineteenth century. In Deerfield there are examples not only of the earlier periods which show English influence but also some most excellent examples of this later work of American inspiration.

THE STEBBINS HOUSE,

DEERFIELD, MASSACHUSETTS.

Built about 1772.

A good example of the embarrassing frequence with which the visitor is confronted with houses that arouse his enthusiasm. Obviously, every house cannot be the "finest" or "most charming" and yet that seems to be what each one is. This particular house probably arouses more futile covetousness on the part of the architecturally inclined visitors than any other building in the town.

**FRONT DOOR DETAIL.
THE HAWKES HOUSE,
DEERFIELD, MASSACHUSETTS.**
Built *circa* 1743.

HOUSE IN WEST STREET, DANBURY, CONNECTICUT. Entrance Detail.

Old Chatham, New York

ONE of the most interesting peculiarities of Early American domestic architecture is its "localism," its adherence to type within the confines, often, of a very restricted locality.

There are, of course, the broad, general divisions of types, or styles, with which we are generally familiar—the domestic architecture of the New England States, of the Middle Atlantic States, and of the South.

These broad divisions, however, would by no means serve to identify all Early American dwellings, because there were sub-styles, and distinctly local styles, many of which were radically at variance with the "typical example."

In the South, for instance, all the great houses did not have classic colonnaded porticoes. Besides the Creole type of the far South (a type absolutely peculiar to the locality), there were a great many differing varieties of the style of the Classic Revival, and there were also the detached houses found in Richmond, Charleston, Norfolk, Annapolis, Alexandria, Baltimore and elsewhere in Delaware, Maryland, Virginia and the Carolinas. All could be classed as "Southern," but there are wide differences in their characteristics.

In the Middle Atlantic States there are the varieties developed by the early pioneer settlers of Pennsylvania as well as by its later more prosperous families. Different, again, is the farmhouse of the Dutch colonists, who built in the northern part of New Jersey, on Staten Island and Long Island, through New York State well up into the Mohawk Valley, and, on the west bank of the Hudson, throughout the Ramapo Hills and the Catskills.

In New England is found further variety, with widely different types, seen in isolated farmhouses and in the substantial homes of the merchants and ship-owners of Salem, Newport and New Bedford.

It is the purpose of this monograph, however, to show how a particular type of house, its identity traceable through detail, appears scattered in an irregular line southward from the Berkshires to the vicinity of Danbury, in Connecticut. And a remarkable proof of the close localism of Early American types of domestic architecture is seen in the fact that the examples illustrated, although found but a few miles from Litchfield, possess characteristics pronouncedly different.

A departure of a few miles from Connecticut is made in the inclusion of the unusually interesting houses in and near Old Chatham, which is over the New York State line due west from Pittsfield and Lenox, and due northwest from Stockbridge and Great Barrington, Massachusetts.

It is permissible, however, to include these old Chatham houses with the Connecticut examples found at Sharon, Kent, Danbury and adjacent townships, because their architectural affinity is at once apparent.

The houses show far more imagination and sophistication in matters of detail than those of Litchfield, the use of Palladian windows being the most conspicuous common feature. Nothing in Litchfield, however, resembles the fine old house at Chatham Center shown in the illustrations.

This house and others included in this monograph show a marked tendency to develop the

Detail of Entablature and Window Head.
HOUSE AT CHATHAM CENTER, NEW YORK.

HOUSE AT CHATHAM CENTER, NEW YORK.

HOUSE AT CHATHAM CENTER, NEW YORK. Detail of Entrance and Front Façade.

design of the entrance by the elaboration of the porch. Fan-lights and side-lights were frequently used, and the Palladian window above the entrance appears to have been the *sine qua non* of the really pretentious house of this type.

It was also a favorite device to plaster the under side of the hood in the forms of cylindrical or elliptical barrel vaults, instead of the plastered quarter-spherical treatment of typical Pennsylvania origin, the "Germantown hood." It would seem, further, that it was the fashion to paint the plaster in these early Connecticut porch-vaults (including the Chatham, New York, examples) a rich shade of blue.

Most interesting of all, however, is a study of the detail of these houses,—detail of which the precedent is lost in obscurity. Certainly some echo of Georgian feeling reached these builders, yet their execution and their departures from academic forms suggest that the Georgian influence was not had at first hand. The bas-relief urns and sunbursts in the frieze of the house at Chatham Center certainly recall the style of the brothers Adam, as does also the strong leaning toward elliptical forms, but the manner in which these are carried out is one of extreme naïveté.

The cornices are distinctly classic in general character, but again depart vigorously from any

147

strict classicism, as is apparent not only in the care-free disregard of the traditional relationship of the members of a classic entablature, but in such quaint vagaries as the continuous fringe of reguli, alternating long and short, with no attempt at triglyphs to relate them to the guttæ of the projection immediately above.

With a thorough knowledge of classic precedents and proportions, it would probably be quite impossible to make the naïve departures from rule which, in the case of these early master-carpenters, were crowned with peculiar success.

For the preservation of these delightful evidences of architectural ingenuousness, it is fortunate that the builders of our early days carried out virtually all their work in white pine, which has held its form without disintegration for the successive decades in which no protective coats of paint have rejuvenated the gray and weather-beaten exteriors.

It is probable, however, the builders of these old houses, especially of those which display a profusion of detail, favored white pine because of the ease with which clear mouldings could be run from it, and because of its receptiveness to the carver's tool.

In the gable end of one of the wings of the Chatham Center house are seen planks of ex-

traordinary width. In many respects this old house affords rich material for study. The treatment of the windows and of the corner pilasters shows a high degree of architectural instinct, when we realize, in the whole house, ample evidence of a lack of academic architectural knowledge. The presence of strong architectural instinct is felt, also, in the whole mass of the house, for no architect of to-day would hesitate to admit that the management of gabled wings, flush with the main façade, is a difficult problem. Few, indeed, would attempt to undertake such a problem, and fewer still would achieve so successful a result.

The Harper house, at Old Chatham, presents a distinctly graceful porch, and another instance of bas-relief sunbursts in the frieze, strangely unrelated to the windows immediately below, but highly interesting in itself.

The third house, found near Old Chatham, is an unusually interesting one, conspicuous, as a "four-square" mass, for its admirably dignified and static proportions. Its siding boards are not lapped, but flush (an unusual detail for this locality), but its detail is closely in character with other houses in the vicinity. The entablature follows a more nearly classic formula, with its frieze detailed in a way to suggest triglyphs and metopes, though reguli are used, almost in

Cornice Detail.
HOUSE AT CHATHAM CENTER, NEW YORK.

BACON HOUSE, KENT, CONNECTICUT.

BACON HOUSE, KENT, CONNECTICUT.

HOUSE AT SHARON, CONNECTICUT.

the manner of dentils, as a purely decorative treatment of the window-heads. The square-headed Palladian window over the porch is excellent in proportion, and well in character with the breadth and amplitude apparent in the whole design.

Travelling southward from Chatham, and back over the State line into Connecticut, but a few miles from Litchfield, Sharon is found to possess a number of very interesting houses. These, for the most part, are more developed in detail than the Litchfield houses.

The embellishment of the frieze, seen in the old house at Chatham, is also apparent in Sharon, the detail of the house above being most effective.

Another interesting frieze treatment is seen in the Bacon house, at Kent, Connecticut—a house also possessing a number of other features. Especially interesting is the little rear porch, with tapered square posts, and the elaborate treatment of all the window-heads. In the frieze, which is carried not only across the gable ends, but up into the peaks as well, there has been an evident intention of following classic precedent in the suggestion of triglyphs, though the alternate spaces are too narrow for metopes. The curious half-circles in the upper part of

these spaces must have been meant to create, by their shadows, the effect of festoons.

At Danbury are found several houses of similar type—especially similar in the general design and detail of the porches. At Sandy Hook, in Connecticut, however, the resemblance swings far more closely toward the kind of house characteristic of Litchfield—plain, clapboarded, sitting close to the grade, and with entrance doors approached only by a broad stone step, and no porch.

Much of the interesting quality of Colonial and Early American domestic architecture, especially in localities remote from the more sophisticated and resourceful cities, came from the fact that nearly all the carpenters and builders in those days were their own architects as well.

There were but few men professionally practicing architecture apart from the actual building of the houses they were designing, and this made possible much of the peculiar kind of individuality characterizing our early domestic architecture.

Perhaps we instinctively admire the successes and ignore the failures of these early builders, which is both a natural and a generous thing to do. Certainly every country builder was by no means gifted with even a faint spark of archi-

BACON HOUSE, KENT, CONNECTICUT.   Detail, Side Doorway.

HARPER HOUSE, OLD CHATHAM, NEW YORK.
Detail of Entrance Porch and Front Façade.

HOUSE AT SANDY HOOK, CONNECTICUT.

HOUSE NEAR SHARON, CONNECTICUT.
"Jackson Farm."

Detail of Entrance.
HOUSE AT SHARON, CONNECTICUT.

tectural genius. Many were downright stupid, but most of them, if we are to judge from their works, were strangely endowed with an inherent sense of architectural fitness.

Not all their detail was developed from books, though such famous works as "The Country Builder's Assistant" had wide popularity. Such forms, however, as may have been found in the "Assistant," and other similar works, are often seen to have been only the basis upon which the more imaginative country builder developed a remarkable variety of individual interpretations.

If these American builders had known more about architectural precedent, or had known less than they did, their works would have been of a nature considerably different from the examples which survive.

But we cannot very well reckon their work in terms of architectural *knowledge;* these early builders had a thing which is, perhaps, rarer to-day—a keen and vigorous architectural *instinct.*

It was this that saved much of their work from being either grotesque or stupid, and which gave it many qualities which could never have been attained through mere architectural knowledge—qualities which afford a wealth and variety of inspiration to those architects of to-day who turn to Early American types for the rendering of the modern American home.

THE FIRST CONGREGATIONAL CHURCH, WEST SPRINGFIELD, MASSACHUSETTS

Built in 1800 to replace first "Church-on-the-Common" built in 1702

DETAIL OF SPIRE

The bell in the tower was recast from the one used in the 1702 church

Western Massachusetts

THE Pilgrim Fathers, by reputation straight-laced and quite given to denying themselves and families many things which would not be termed extravagances by moderns, had many redeeming qualities, among them a shrewd and calculating intelligence and unquenchable ambition.

The Connecticut Valley settlers, once in possession of their rugged and somewhat threatening promised land, were for only a short time content with their primitive shelters and hastily thrown-together barricades. Some of their earliest buildings suggest the severe outlines of such structures as the gloomy gaol in that old Chelmsford-Springfield whence came many settlers of this region. That is, from the town, not the gaol!

The proper cultivation of newly-cleared land, and study of the elements necessary to make it produce food in the shortest possible space of time interested these pioneers far more at that time than what style of house would best suit each man's particular corner of the lovely New England landscape. Their sterling women-folk were undoubtedly prime and potent factors in the inevitable reaction. Windows here, conveniences for housekeeping there, enlargements of space in first one direction, then another, and most of them suggested by necessity. These changes increased with the lessening of danger from terrors by night and arrows by day. The tendency toward lines of beauty in

building at first showed itself as a matter of course, with the wealthier immigrants, whom their neighbors were not slow to imitate. Ornament as well as utility was added as each settler prospered and felt that he could afford to do so. The decades swiftly passed and it can not be denied that now-existing examples of western New England home-building possess many features of artistic as well as purely architectural charm.

Among leaf-embowered homesteads on each side of Longmeadow's principal street—a veritable "royal greensward, fit for camp of kings"—one of the glimpses longest remembered by tourists with an eye for sheer beauty of setting, is the Alexander Field house.

Anciently the Indian "Massacksic," this was "land to be desired" indeed! It was this same broad, ample stretch of "ye longe meddowe" lying next south of the 1636 Springfield plantation, which attracted the shrewd settlers. It should be recorded that they very early showed signs of appreciation of beautiful home-site surroundings, and were ill-content with lands mainly suitable for farming.

Quaint old records show how, in 1703, Daniel, Benjamin and Lieut. Joseph Cooley and a dozen neighbors in the lowlands next the "Greate River" petitioned the parent town for leave to possess home-lots on "Convenient and better land out of the general field, on the hil," because floods have "put oᵣ Lives in grt Danger, oᵣ housing much damnifyed, & many cattle are Lost." The Alexander Field house stands upon the original six-lot grant assigned to the Cooleys.

DETAIL OF FRONT DOORWAY—THE BOICE (RICE) HOUSE, AMHERST, MASSACHUSETTS

This grant extended for 120 rods along the ancient "commons" highway, laid out 330 feet wide—and almost as far back towards the river. The Field family arrived in Longmeadow about 1728, and through marriages with the Cooleys came into possession of the site near the head of magnificent Longmeadow Street.

Scarcely a mile in a bee line (thrice that around by nearest bridge way) lies the eldest settlement of western Massachusetts, Agawam; first choice of the pioneers as a site for Springfield. The first dwelling in this region erected by white man was the rough shelter placed in the famous "House meadow" at the north end of Agawam, by William Pynchon's henchmen, Cable and Woodcock, in the summer of 1635. It was abandoned within the year because of the danger from

floods; and the Springfield River bank was for the next two centuries the heart of "town," since 'twas ever best to be on the safer side. It is architecturally interesting to note in passing that the next year's record states that this house was "built at the common charge for six pounds!"

In the heart of the old town, on the east side of the wide, elm-arched street where, on the afternoon of June 30, 1775, General Washington passed, bound for Cambridge where the new Continental Army awaited its commander-in-chief, stands the fine old Leonard dwelling built in 1808. Both upstairs and down, the middle section of the house is all hallway, about twelve by forty feet, with handsome panelled doors leading into ample rooms on each side. Some of the big fireplace openings have the wide flagging hearthstones fitted into the flooring, the latter still containing many of the original broad boards. On the ground floor the doors, cut in half, allowed the serving of flip and cider over the lower closed part. "Side-fire" bake-ovens, hand-wrought door-latches, and nail-heads, and hand-hewn foundation timbers are interesting features of this one of the most substantial houses of its era in Agawam. A curious detail of the side door is the hinged halving, from top to bottom rather than the frequent side-to-side treatment. Old residents aver that the latch-half of the door was opened mainly to answer inquiries; and that the full forty inches of opening was thrown wide when answers and inquiries proved satisfactory to all concerned.

West Springfield, which once included in its twelve-mile length both Agawam and Holyoke is now separated from the former by the Agawam River. In the eastern edge of its central part, on a lordly location overlooking miles of Connecticut River valley, and directly across the river from Dr. J. G. Holland's famous "Brightwood", stands the old First Congregational Church, the corner stone of which is marked "June, 1800." The townspeople of that day had long been dissatisfied with the primitive "church-on-the-common," forty-two feet square and built a century before that. John Ashley, a prosperous parishioner, see-

THE BOICE (RICE) HOUSE, SOUTH PLEASANT STREET, AMHERST, MASSACHUSETTS
FRONT ELEVATION   *Built by Horace Kellogg about* 1828

ing the inhabitants could not agree upon a location for a more modern building, terminated a long and rather violent controversy on the question, by coming forward with an offer of thirteen hundred pounds on condition that the "spacious and elegant meeting house" of the photographs should be placed "on a spot designated by me": and thus the old "white church on the hill" came into being, where all the different factions of town could look up to it. It was built "on honor" as well as on a foundation of red sandstone; and its hand-hewn timbers of white oak are found to be sound and staunch to this day. The very young contractor, Captain Timothy Billings of Deerfield, aged twenty-eight! received about $1400—part of it in St. Croix rum—for building it. Ashley and Billings, consulting with the famous Dr. Lathrop, who was then minister of the church, were responsible for its architecture, which has been greatly admired. In style it is a rather less severely simple modification of the Christopher Wren pattern,

Detail of Side Doorway

THE CHARLES LEONARD HOUSE, AGAWAM CENTER, MASSACHUSETTS
Built in 1808 by Chas. Leonard, a farmer-graduate of Harvard, at one end of his great farm

examples of which are quite numerous in New England.

Another condition made by the donor of the money for this church was that the building should be used as a church for a hundred years. After a full century, plus a dozen years more for good measure, it was sold to become a Masonic temple; and another church building was adopted close to the historic spot where the ancient building of controversy had been established. Sacred relics of the beautiful old church on the hill, such as carved ornaments from the sides of its high square pulpit, and panelled pew doors, have been built into some of the houses of the neighborhood, as a reminder of the "Mt. Orthodox" that used to be!

Old Hadley, and that newer part long known as East Hadley—which is now Amherst—have some charming old dwellings, with the hip and gambrel roof as well as fan-light suggestions of the good taste and imagination of the elders in architecture. The houses were first of all built to withstand the rigors of the once savage New England winters, and moreover were built to last. They blossom out, unexpectedly, into fanciful bits of ornamentation here and there, some perhaps accidental, but many more by design.

The old Boice place, on South Pleasant Street, Amherst, now owned and occupied by the Rice family, is one of the particularly noteworthy specimens of late eighteenth century home-building. It was built about 1828 by the farmer-carpenter, Horace Kellogg. That he was a man of uncommonly good judgment becomes apparent when it is known that he was on the building committee having in charge the erection of the much-admired third building of the First Congregational Church; the same which was transformed into what is now the stately College Hall. Other specimens of the Kellogg taste in such matters are found elsewhere in the eastern part of Hampshire County in buildings which not only wear but look well with which he had to do either as a builder or in an advisory capacity. The family of Sanford Boice, by which the place is now generally known, occupied it for the first twenty years of the present century.

The Hubbard house in Northampton, so called from one of its earlier owners, was built in 1744 by a grandson of Cornet Joseph Parsons to whom the original grant of land was made and who was slain by the Indians of King Philip in 1675. As a precaution against Indian attack by day (the last recorded tragedy from this source was the killing of Elisha Clark of Northampton, August 1747) strong wooden shutters were placed in front of each first floor window.

THE CHARLES LEONARD HOUSE, AGAWAM CENTER, MASSACHUSETTS

Built in 1808 *on the Agawam Commons*

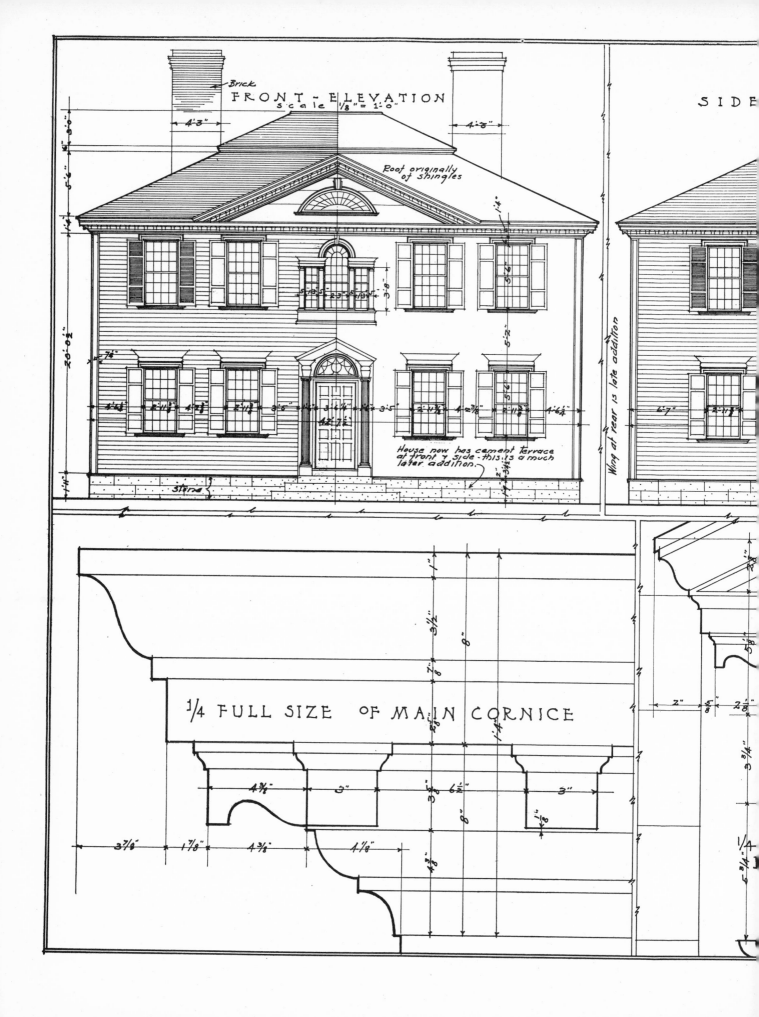

FRONT - ELEVATION
scale 1/8" = 1'-0"

SIDE

Brick

Roof originally
of shingles

House now has cement terrace
at front & side - this is a much
later addition.

Wing at rear is late addition

Storns

1/4 FULL SIZE OF MAIN CORNICE

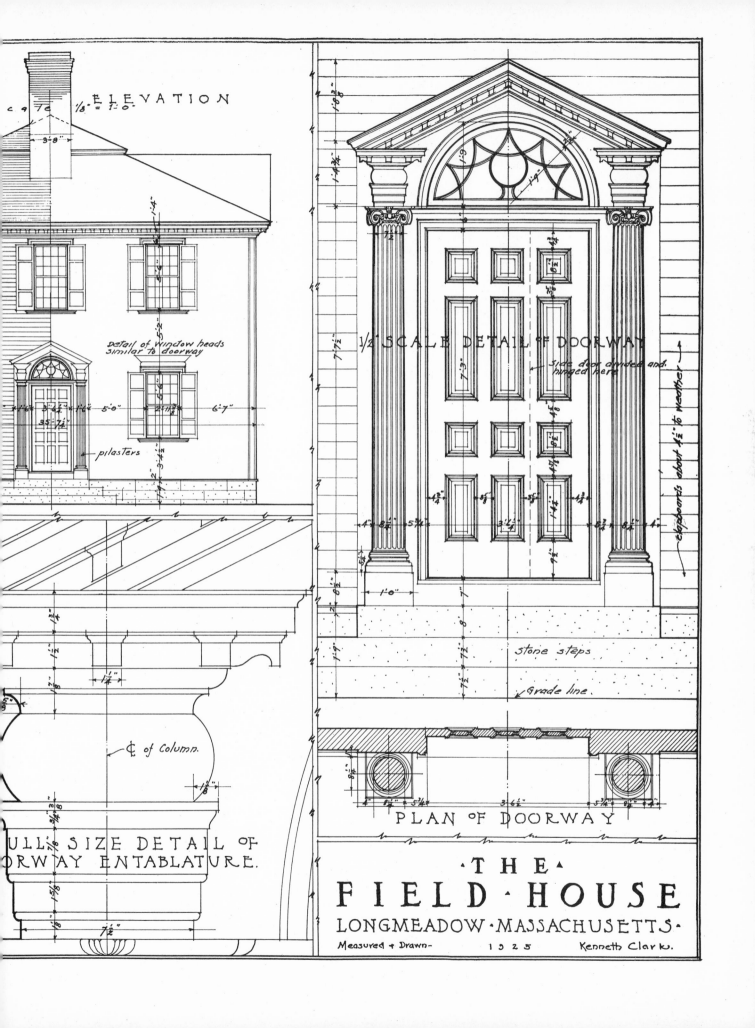

ELEVATION

⅛" = 1'-0"

c. 970

9'-8"

Detail of window heads
similar to doorway

pilasters

½ SCALE DETAIL OF DOORWAY

Side door divided and
hinged here

clapboards about 4½" to weather

stone steps

Grade line.

℄ of Column.

FULL SIZE DETAIL OF
DOORWAY ENTABLATURE.

PLAN OF DOORWAY

·THE·
FIELD·HOUSE
LONGMEADOW·MASSACHUSETTS·

Measured + Drawn-   1925   Kenneth Clark.

DETAIL OF ENTABLATURE—FRONT DOORWAY

THE FIELD HOUSE
LONGMEADOW
MASSACHUSETTS

MEASURED DRAWINGS *from*
The George F. Lindsay Collection

THE FIELD HOUSE, LONGMEADOW, MASSACHUSETTS

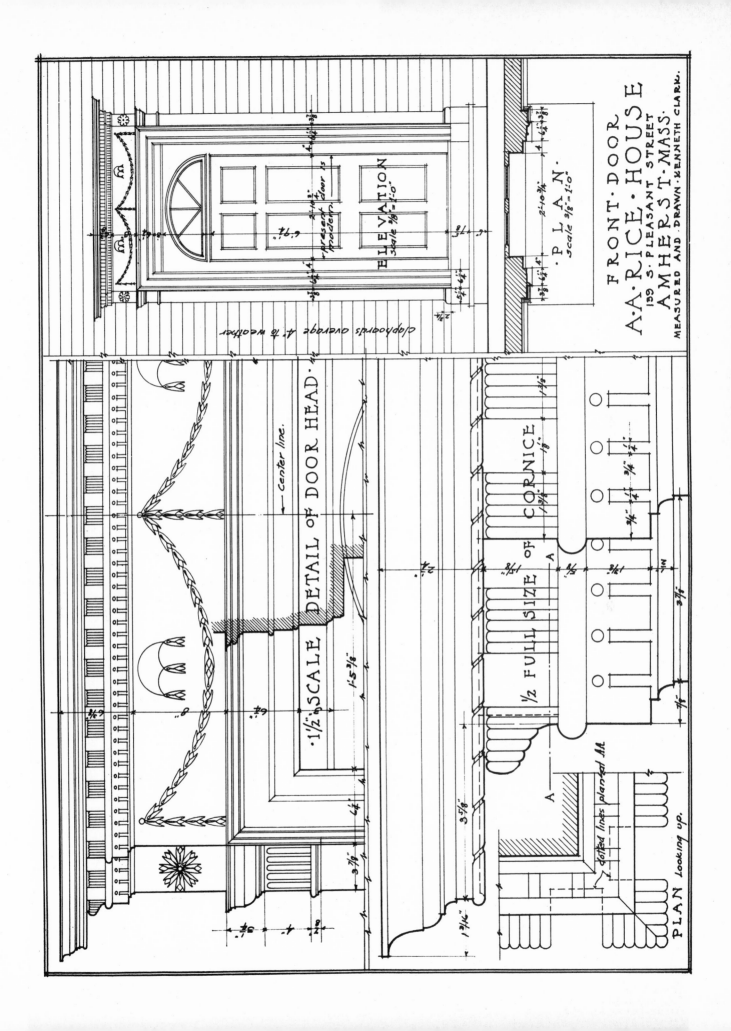

FRONT·DOOR
A·A·RICE·HOUSE
159 S·PLEASANT·STREET
AMHERST·MASS.
MEASURED AND DRAWN·KENNETH CLARK.

·PLAN·
Scale 3/8"=1'-0"

ELEVATION
Scale 3/8"=1'-0"

present door is modern

clapboards average 4" to weather

DETAIL OF DOOR HEAD
·1½"·SCALE

Center line

½ FULL SIZE OF CORNICE

dotted lines planted AA

PLAN looking up.

CENTRAL MOTIVE

THE FIELD HOUSE,
LONGMEADOW, MASSACHUSETTS

THE FIELD HOUSE,
LONGMEADOW, MASSACHUSETTS

Detail of Central Portion of Main Facade

DOORWAY OF THE SERGEANT HOUSE, STOCKBRIDGE, MASSACHUSETTS
In 1734, John Sergeant of Yale commenced preaching to the peaceful Indian tribe in Stockbridge meadows

Berkshires Architecture

THE wooden buildings of the Berkshire towns and villages—and nearly all the older buildings are of wood—are to be found peculiarly interesting and illuminating instances that not only afford an architectural chronicle of that portion of Massachusetts, but also serve to point a moral that architects and laymen alike may very well apply to their profit.

It has been the fortune of many of the Berkshire towns to lie upon important arteries of travel, that is to say, the arteries of travel as they were ordered in the days of the stage coach, when the various centers of population within our particular field most chiefly attained their growth. This fact meant that they were especially accessible to every new influence from the outside world, and that the character of the buildings erected as the years passed assumed a sort of cosmopolitan catholicity of expression that plainly proclaimed how ready the Berkshire people were

to accept and adopt each phase of style as it arose to dominate the course of design. There are early 18th Century examples richly reminiscent in their motifs and details of those robust Baroque interpretations of the Classic mode handed down from the days of Sir Christopher Wrenn and his immediate followers. There are severely urban reminders of that somewhat later era when austere, academic Palladianism held sway and meticulous solicitude for ancient precedent was not confined to dilettante and professional purists, but permeated the whole social consciousness of the period and affected the country architect-carpenters in varying degree, according to their understandings and nimbleness of perception. In the next succeeding epoch the seed of Adam inspiration fell on fertile soil, and produced a plentiful crop of delicacies and refinements characteristic of that age. Then manifestations of Neo-Classicism in turn gave place to a newer era with Roman mode that drew

THE SERGEANT HOUSE, STOCKBRIDGE, MASS.
Built early in the 18th Century

Early 18th Century Doorway
HOUSE AT STOCKBRIDGE, MASS.

architectural forms in great numbers and with a perfection that stamps the growth as unmistakably of a certain period. In other towns or villages, when prosperity came late, the evidences of later affluence are reflected with equal distinctness in the local architecture. Unfortunately, some places where the early or later 18th Century types had flourished with charming results, received a fresh impetus of wealth, in the mid-19th Century and those phenomina bore deadly fruit in an appalling crop of alterations and additions so that the original character of the houses was either wholly obliterated or else marred beyond any reasonable hope of restoration. Extra gables with jig-saw barge boards; new front doors of stock mill pattern, with single plate glass lights filling the entire upper half; the wholesale destruction of the window glazing and the substitution of soleless negative sashes with large panes; the bursting forth of irrelevant bay windows; the contrivance of still more irrelevant door hoods supported on fearfully and wonderfully made brackets fretted with all the labyrinthine contortions of the industrious

its being and forms partly from the current Regency style in England and partly from the creations of the Directoire and early Empire in France. This suave and pleasant Anglo-French blending gradually yielded to the fully developed types of the Greek Revival. The complete record lies open to be read in the Berkshire towns. What has been said of dwelling houses in this connection also holds good with reference to structures erected for civil or public purposes.

To understand this comprehensive collection of successive types, one must remember what has already been pointed out—that the constant contact of the Berkshire towns and villages with the outside world ensured not only susceptibility but also a warm welcome to each influence as it arrived. The Berkshire towns were unlike so many other New England towns that displayed with singular nicety some one type of architectural development and became classics for the particular style that dominated their streets. For example, when prosperity and affluence came early, we find a great number of houses exhibit contemporary

Early 18th Century Doorway
HOUSE AT GREAT BARRINGTON, MASS.

but misguided jig-saw artist,—these and similar achievements of mid-Victorian mauling and man-handling, to say nothing of even more ruthless, more far-reaching vandalism have left their indelible trail of horrid ruin.

The Berkshire towns, it is true, suffered their share of calamities and accidents during the era of unenlightenment, but they have managed to

tations for which the local architect-carpenters were wholly responsible. Their work cannot be considered in the light of an adroit exhibition of slavish archæology display. It was very far from it. It was replete with native vitality whether the manifold differences of expression encountered were due to an imperfect understanding of the original prototypes; an insufficient acquaint-

THE LENOX ACADEMY BUILDING, LENOX, MASSACHUSETTS
Built in 1803

preserve intact a great deal that is well worth while—enough to retain their character and afford instances of architectural excellence and elegance that ought not to be overlooked in any survey of wooden architecture.

What makes the study of the early wooden architecture both engaging and valuable is the diversity of interpretations to be found, interpre-

ance with the architectural books of the period, or whether they were begotten of the promptings of ingenuity and ignorant mother wit when working with materials different from those employed in the Classic originals, it would be difficult to say. One is inclined to believe that both factors played their parts in the evolution that translated the forms of wood and stone into wood. At any rate,

THE LENOX ACADEMY BUILDING, LENOX, MASSACHUSETTS
Dating from 1803, *formerly a famous classical school and now a private school for small children*

HOUSE AT RICHMOND, MASSACHUSETTS. (WEST OF LENOX MOUNTAIN)
Built in late 18th Century, in town named in honor of the Duke of Richmond

what we of today see is that the builders of the 18th and early 19th Centuries had mastered the vocabulary of domestic architecture in the Classic modes, but spoke the language with a local accent. And all these local variations stamped with individuality the several places where they occurred, for in no two areas do we find precisely the same evidences of originality in adaptations. In one neighborhood it may be a particular type of doorway; in another, an unusual type of gable end window may arrest attention. Oftentimes, within the bounds of a small area, it is possible to trace the activities of a single architect-carpenter by little peculiarities in the handling of certain details that he had left spread about on this house or on that, like trade-marks. Those little features are mere mannerisms without falling into the category of affectations. As an example of this sort of thing, we may point to the oft repeated use of the so-called Palladian window as an attic light within the peak of the gable end, in a great number of houses where the boundaries of New York, Connecticut and Massachusetts meet just at the foot of the Berkshire Hills.

Notwithstanding the quasi-cosmopolitan character of wooden architecture in the Berkshire

ENTRANCE DETAIL—THE FRY HOUSE, RICHMOND, MASSACHUSETTS

towns, a fact to which attention has already been drawn, the same impulse toward individualistic interpretation was actively at work, just as it was in more secluded neighborhoods where one tradition was strongly entrenched. One of the most conspicuous evidences of this tendency to develop local mannerisms and diverting conceits is seen in the frequent employment of a semi-elliptical gable end window above a pilastered plinth. In Great Barrington and several other places the leaded glazing of these attic lights assumes divers pleasing patterns. But even the local mannerisms exhibited many variations within its restricted area. In the pediment of the little bank at Stock-

ENTRANCE DETAIL—THE PERRY HOUSE, RICHMOND, MASSACHUSETTS

THE PRESIDENT'S HOUSE, WILLIAMS COLLEGE, WILLIAMSTOWN, MASSACHUSETTS

GREEK "TEMPLE" HOUSE, WEST STOCKBRIDGE, MASS.

bridge the semi-ellipse on a pilastered plinth appears merely as a decorative motif and a very effective one at that. There is no light in the half-ellipse, but instead a wooden fan or sunburst device with vigorously modelled divergent rays. Sometimes, too, the semi-ellipse was converted into a semi-circle above a plinth and was either glazed or filled with a rayed motif. The employment of these conceits kept its hold on the imagination for a long time, for we find it in the pediment of the Neo-Grec house at West Stockbridge

THE PRESIDENT'S HOUSE, WILLIAMS COLLEGE, WILLIAMSTOWN, MASSACHUSETTS

and even after ellipses went out of fashion, the tradition of an attic light on a plinth persisted, for not a few fully developed Greek Revival

LATE 18th CENTURY HOUSE AT FLAT BROOK, MASSACHUSETTS

BANK IN STOCKBRIDGE, MASS.

"temple" houses display a very rigid rectangular leaded light above a plinth. The changes are many in every form of this device, but the conception back of it is unchanged. Thus we have variety in unity not only in the manifold sum total of the Berkshire wooden architecture, with its procession of related styles, but also in the adapting of a conception, partly decorative, partly utilitarian, to employment in varied environments.

In all of the Berkshire houses almost without exception, the plan is perfectly obvious. A rectangle, sometimes with, sometimes without an ell extension at the rear, and simply and logically divided into the requisite rooms and halls without attempting any unusual or ingenious devices or arrangements. Even to the very urban houses built at the end of the 18th Century or in the early years of the 19th Century, full of Adam elegancies so far as their exteriors were concerned, there was no disposition to indulge in elliptical rooms, circular halls or oval stairwells. In houses presenting such exteriors as those at Richmond or at Flat Brook one might expect to discover an occasional flight of this sort. But there were none. The utmost departure from a strictly rectangular plan consisted in a one story wing at one or both sides of the main mass of the house.

Although the Berkshire architect-carpenter employed the different phases of the Classic mode very largely as a repertoire of external decoration, using the more organic features only at a comparatively late date and in a very conservative manner then, their achievements have a lesson to teach us, the lesson of flexibility. While ardently admiring Classic forms and ever ready to make use of them to the fullest extent they were not purists. They did not scruple to combine and modify details in a way that would have made the British worshippers of Palladio rave with anguish. And yet, they often did it so well and with such consummate delicacy and interest that one cannot cavil at the liberties they took. Indeed, the exercise of their self-appointed license and independence of action made the Classic mode a vital thing. Their "jumbling" has supplied a precedent that more than one architect of our own day and generation has turned to account with happy effect.

And now for the moral of our tale. A recent survey of the field of domestic architecture plainly shows that an ever increasing number of people are demanding houses of a distinctly romantic type rather than houses of Classic mould. The reason is not far to seek. Too many architects and too many laymen seem to have the idea that all that is necessary in order to design a house of the Classic type is to create a rectangular mass, poke the requisite number of fenestrations in for doors and windows and then hang on an appropriate "*quantum sufficit*" of hackneyed details. The result of such an unworthy conception must inevitably be stupid and repellent. People crave variety as a modicum of individuality. The craving is natural and perfectly justifiable. But if they build and live in houses of the type just alluded to, houses turned out by the dozen with standardized stupidity, they can have neither variety nor individuality. Consequently they turn to the romantic school to satisfy their cravings.

But the Classic mode has just as much vitality as it ever had. The trouble is with the sodden folly of those who conceive it to be what has just been pointed out. The early builders and adapters succeeded in achieving endless interest and engaging variety, while adhering to the general unity of the Classic traditions. If the Classic style is to continue as a vital factor in domestic architecture, it must be rescued from the unworthy opinion formed of it by those insufficiently acquainted with all its varied possibilities. There can be no better corrective for the notion of monotony attaching to this time-honored fashion than a close study of what the architect-carpenter of a bygone day did in the Berkshire towns dominated by the tradition of wooden architecture.

FRONT GATE AND FENCE,
FRY HOUSE, RICHMOND, MASSACHUSETTS

THE ISAAC ROYALL HOUSE AT MEDFORD, MASS.
The East Front, now facing the street.   Built in 1732 along the lines of a "nobleman's house" in Antigua.   An unusual feature is the horizontal emphasis obtained from the treatment of the windows.

THE CUSHING HOUSE AT HINGHAM, MASS.

Built in the early part of the 18th century, probably in 1730;
a good example of the simple farmhouse type.

18th Century New England

THE early architecture of New England is, for the most part, distinctive for its simplicity and economy, both of plan and construction. It was based, in the first instance, upon rooms of small size and low height, and was as easy to erect and furnish as to heat and defend from enemies, climatic and human. The construction was a simple framework, whose principal supports—generally either of oak or white pine—were hewn from native timber and framed in the fashion the early colonists previously had been accustomed to in England. These timbers were also spaced with an economy in use that permitted the spaces between to be spanned with small irregular pieces of timber and boarding; just as the non-supporting partitions were, in turn, most frequently composed of roughly shaped plank. These heavy timbers once settled into place, the walls could be strengthened against arrows or cold by a further protective filling of brick or tile, so often disclosed when old dwellings are torn down. In one place only was the scale invariably ample and generous; and this was around the central chimney, always the feature of the house.

In the early Colonial cottage again, little, if any, attempt was made for mere ornament or decoration. Recollections of Euro-

ENTRANCE DETAIL

pean craftsmanship were adapted to new conditions with little apparent trouble, and with what we now realize to have been greatly successful common sense. When these structures have remained unaltered by succeeding generations, they are rarely anything but beautiful in their direct outlines and sturdy proportions; the composition of sky-line and chimney with the ground contour, and the grouping and proportions of the wall openings being always notably successful. Occasionally these early carpenters, in an entrance doorway, a mantel, or perhaps in the staircase, would seize the chance to apply their craft-knowledge with a little more freedom from restraint, and while the results may sometimes seem to us perhaps a bit *naïve* or quaintly obvious, at other times one cannot help but acknowledge they display as superb an acquaintance with, and appreciation of, beauty in line, detail and in the placing and modeling of ornament as any inventions of other and more sophisticated days.

The earliest type of plan had undoubtedly a room on each side of an entrance, a staircase placed in front of a central chimney, and a kitchen, located perhaps partly in a rear shed or ell.

Such an arrangement is ordinarily regarded as of the "farmhouse" type, and is sufficiently familiar hardly to

FRONT ELEVATION. THE DOAK HOUSE, MARBLEHEAD, MASS.

THE TYLER HOUSE AT WAYLAND, MASS.

Built previous to 1725

A typical example of a farmhouse with a room on each side of entrance and a central chimney.

**THE SHUTE HOUSE
AT HINGHAM, MASS.**

Detail of Side Entrance

A house of unusual type, built about 1762.

THE OLD BEMIS HOUSE, WATERTOWN, MASS.
Built about 1750

THE STEARNS HOUSE,
BEDFORD, MASS.

Built from a design by
Reuben Duren, Architect.

require illustration. If such· is to be supplied, a typical example is found in the Cushing House at Hingham, or the old "Tyler House" at Wayland, standing on the old prehistoric Indian "Bay-Path." This latter house dates from the early part of the 18th century (sometime previous to 1725) and is now deserted. At the rear the roof of this house now sweeps down, nearly to the ground, in the usual fashion, being unbroken for any purposes of light or ventilation. As originally built, the house undoubtedly consisted of four rooms only: two below and two above. As it now stands, the kitchen runs the full width of the ell, and is located exactly in the center, behind the chimney, with a small room behind the front room on the left of the entrance: the

WINDOW DETAIL. JUDGE JOSEPH LEE HOUSE. CAMBRIDGE, MASS.

space at the right being taken up by closets and the side entrance. The original frame is of hewn oak, covered with one thickness of weatherboards beveled on the edges to overlap without lathing or plastering, but with the timber frame filled in with soft burned brick. Another indication of the age of this house is the abrupt "over-hang" or projection at the eaves line, without soffit molding or any other suggestion of the later "cornice" treatment.

There are to be found only a very few instances of a house of interestingly different type, where the chimney and staircase occur at one end instead of in the center, leaving but one room across the front. Such a type appears in the little Southborough house, where the typical projected

THE JOHN DOCKRAY HOUSE, WAKEFIELD, R. I.

Built in the early part of the 18th century.

face-gable showing at the end indicates how naturally the early builders adapted their plan to get the outlook and sun desired in rear rooms.

In this house there existed a curious detail of construction in the window-caps, intended to protect the top of the window-case, which was projected beyond the frame of the building and applied to its face in the old-fashioned way. These molded caps were crowned by a sloping member, carefully hewn and shaped from one heavy log of wood so as to provide a sloping "wash" across the top and front and returned on the two ends; while the carpenter took pains to leave a standing flange at the back over which the siding was broken, thus providing a sort of flashing, but executed entirely in wood!

OLD FRONT DOOR, SHUTE HOUSE.
HINGHAM, MASS.

Later in the 18th century, the American builders began to secure the "Carpenter's Handbooks," first published in England about 1756, and from these they developed new details far more easily, merely adapting them to the somewhat simplified conditions and requirements of the American village or town in which they lived and worked. Later, the demand for these practical builders' assistants became so great that at least one volume was reprinted in this country; being compiled and issued by a certain Asher Benjamin, an architect in Greenfield, Massachusetts, in 1797.

For a number of years the plan developed a few changes, except in so far as they were demanded by special or larger requirements imposed by the owner. The house below is of this

A GOOD EXAMPLE OF AN EARLY FARMHOUSE
Illustrating shingle ends combined with clapboarding on the front.

THE SHUTE HOUSE, HINGHAM, MASS.

West Doorway
"THE LINDENS," DANVERS, MASS.
Built in 1745

Front Doorway
AN OLD HOUSE, HINGHAM, MASS.
Built about 1760

A small part of this house, built in 1631, is the oldest section of any house now standing in America. The principal portion of the mansion was not, however, built until 1732. The exterior of the front and back of this house is in the original White Pine.

THE ROYALL HOUSE, MEDFORD, MASS.   Built in 1732

simple type, save that it presents the less usual composition of one window on one side the center door balanced by two upon the other; the single window being four lights wide (or twenty panes in all) where the others are of three wide, or fifteen lights.

A very ancient house indeed was the old Doak house at Marblehead, which unfortunately has disappeared. Aside from the simplicity —almost the crudity— of the execution of its architectural details, the age of this building is evidenced by many other indications only to be recognized by the architect or antiquarian. Nevertheless, its definite attitude of dignity, of aloofness, should be apparent to any passer-by, and it is this quality, sometimes, as much as any other, that arouses our admiration for these early Colonial masterpieces. They achieve so perfect, if unconscious, a relation of parts—the proportion of opening to wall space and of glass division; the architraves around the opening to window area; the cornice to the roof design and the wall height— that it often seems impossible to improve the structure as a whole. Even though single details sometimes appear crudely executed by local workmen, it yet remains an open question whether mere improvement in execution or in refinement —if attempted—would be as well related, and harmonize as well with the complete design.

The gambrel roof type— always difficult to proportion —was used by the early builders with the greatest freedom, and with a perfect sense for the right relation of parts. Sometimes the gambrel is flattened and ample in proportion, at others the gable appears more restricted and the proportions made for greater dignity and height. It is this latter aspect that is more appropriately found on the larger houses to which this variation of the roof of Mansart was occasionally applied, although undoubtedly it was then, as now, best adapted to enlarge the living space available on the second floor.

OLD FARMHOUSE, SOUTHBOROUGH, MASS.

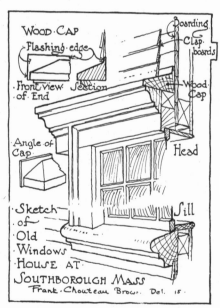

The Wadsworth House, sometimes called the President's House, on the grounds of Harvard University, while of much larger size— crowding three stories and an attic under its capacious roof beams—has a gambrel of very nearly the proportion of the modest cape cottages. The walls of this house were "raised" on May 24, 1726, although the side doorway, the ell, and the two one-story additions made on each end are of later dates.

In the very well known Royall House in Medford were, besides the slave quarters and the portion shown in the photographs, two ells, one of which may have been the earlier farmhouse that stood upon this site. One of these ells was burned only a few years ago. It is supposed that the original farmhouse built here by Governor Winthrop, soon after the settlement of Medford in 1630, was incorporated into the dwelling later built by John Usher, after he came into possession of the place in 1677.

Despite its unaccustomed surroundings, the Shirley-Eustis Home in Roxbury stands, only slightly removed from its original site, as dignified today as when it was first built. An old newspaper of 1865 proclaiming a sale of the house's contents gives the date as 1743; and adds the information that it was built of oak framed in England and of imported brick—although three different sizes are now to be found. The house was purchased by Governor Eustis in 1819, and it may be that he added the two porches at either end which have now disappeared, but which were so seldom found on early houses in the New England Colonies. This house also has two fronts; and, as in the Royall House, the driveway front again proves to be of the more interest architecturally.

Although a little later than the middle of the century, the Shute House at Hingham is so interesting a type as to require consideration here. The lot was bought in 1754 and the house built by 1762, and the ell is of later date.

THE WADSWORTH HOUSE, CAMBRIDGE, MASS.   Built in 1726

The way the front clapboards extend by and beyond the clapboarding across the end gable, without corner boards or other finish of any kind, should be noted.

"ELMWOOD," RESIDENCE OF JAMES RUSSELL LOWELL, CAMBRIDGE, MASSACHUSETTS.   Detail of Front.

The door itself is of recent inspiration, and some parts of the entrance feature are executed in new woodwork. How far they exactly reproduce the original, it is of course impossible to determine. This photograph clearly shows the omission of corner boards and treatment of siding at the angles.

Three-Story New England Houses

THE Colonial dwellings of New England group themselves naturally into three definite physical classifications. There is first the small cottage one story and a half high, an early and more primitive type found in the smaller and less wealthy communities or in the country. This kind of cottage is typical of certain sections, such as part of Maine and Cape Cod; and certain fisher villages, such as Biddeford Pool, Marblehead, portions of Gloucester and other towns. Some of these cottages are essentially charming, but they possess little value except the incidental detail for most architectural work of the current day.

There is, secondly, the larger house of two stories and roof, containing generally an attic story. This house may be of the simplest possible type of pitch roof with end gable, typical of the larger farmstead; or, in order to provide more space on the third floor, the gable may be developed in the familiar gambrel roof. Or, this same type of house may itself easily extend into the larger, more spacious and pretentious abode of the landed proprietor, wealthy merchantman or shipowner, where we find the most beautiful architectural details that, for delicacy, refinement and restraint, have not elsewhere been equalled under any other conditions on this continent and never surpassed.

In New England there was little tendency to develop the type of mansion familiar throughout the South. The central house with extended wings on both sides is rarely found, except in some uncommon instances, such as the Black House at Ellsworth, or the Governor Gore mansion outside of Boston. On the other hand, the unbalanced development of a big house with one wing is very often seen, particularly in such sections, for instance, as the Old Providence Plantations, or in Salem, or wherever considerable wealth had come into the possession of the leading merchants or families of that time. In these more crowded and larger Colonial cities, however, this wing extension generally developed at the back of the main house—rather than extended parallel with the street frontage—and there it often grew until it produced a well-defined enclosure surrounding a servants' courtyard at the back or one side of the main house. This tendency is definitely indicated in the Royall House, and even more clearly in some of the old Providence and Portland houses, or the Pierce-Nichols house at Salem, for instance. While the New England mansion of this type developed many interesting details of handling, its general exterior architectural treatment remained nevertheless fairly balanced and formal, and, within the rigid outlines prescribed by custom, no very great variation of design or *parti* was possible. It therefore came naturally to be that, when in New England a still larger dwelling was demanded by conditions, it rather took the form of the three-story house than attempted to extend a second ell or wing to balance the one formerly thrown out,—and this type of dwelling, possessing peculiar architectural difficulties of its own for solution, came soon to be recognized as a third principal, characteristic type that distinguished some of the later houses of New England that were generally built just previous to, or immediately after, the year 1800. That the type was not exclusively to be found in any one locality is proved by the accompanying illustrations, which have been selected purposely to illustrate the considerable geographical area from which the material was drawn, and have intentionally avoided reproducing any of the most familiar and well-known three-story structures in Salem, or selecting more than one or two of the most important or suggestive examples from Portsmouth, Portland, or the other larger New England communities.

The problem of undertaking to increase the Colonial house to three stories in height and retain its usual and nearly square proportions in plan, is one that might well cause the architectural designer to pause and carefully regard the difficulties presented by the problem of making such a box-like structure attractive and consistent with his Colonial ideals. Such a square and uncompromising house as the old Haven homestead at Portsmouth, for instance, contains little architectural relief from its rectangular proportions except such as is to be found in the caps of the windows, the delicate arched detail of the very broad and overhanging cornice, and the balustrade, that, in the case of the porch at least, has every suggestion of being a more modern addition to the design. Here the original builders evidently felt that they could do no less than make a virtue of necessity and so give to the porch and doorway all the emphasis of dignity and height that the house façade made possible, their only attempt at diminishing the height being found in the low third-story windows, only two panes of glass high.

The Woodbury mansion near Portsmouth indicates a more conscientious endeavor to relieve the box-like exterior proportions of the dwelling by the horizontal bands, the increase in height of the first and second story windows, and the balconies used across the front. Again, dignity and simplicity, with great refinement of proportion, are indicated,—particularly in the details of the porch, where the balustrade is even more obviously a modern addition, although the roof balustrade with its halved balusters seems more consistently to belong to the original design. This house is greatly favored by setting in a rather beautiful grove, where the unkempt terraces and tree surroundings add greatly to its interest and attractiveness.

At Danversport still stands an old house, much battered by wind and weather in its exposed location, of less depth in plan than is usual with the three-story house, and with far more than the usual chaste beauty of refinement and simplicity in design and proportion. Seen as it appears in these photographs, without blinds or shutters, and largely minus paint, it nevertheless commands attention and respect from these very sterling qualities of a majestic consciousness of innate beauty and serenity of proportion and refinement of detail.

Rather earlier in date than most of these other houses (as indicated by its bold and virile moulding section and heavy window caps) is Elmwood in Cambridge. With the fenestration rather more gracefully composed, and with only what adventitious and incidental element of balance is obtained from the porch on one side and the one-story service wing on the other, this house ventures sturdily to win approbation solely by means of the rather unusual treatment of entrance and second-story window overhead, —which, in its present form at least, is largely a conjectural reproduction of what may have been its original design.

THE HAVEN HOUSE
PORTSMOUTH, NEW HAMPSHIRE.

Built about 1800.

Built by Nathan Reed between 1798, when he purchased this part of Governor Endicott's old "Orchard Farm," and 1803, when he finished his term in Congress. The house was afterward owned by Captain Crowingshield and Captain Benjamin Porter. In the pond in front of the dwelling the first owner experimented with a paddle-wheel steamboat.

"ELMWOOD," RESIDENCE OF JAMES RUSSELL LOWELL, CAMBRIDGE, MASSACHUSETTS.

This house is supposed originally to have been built (in what was then old Watertown) either by John Stratton in 1760 or by Colonel Thomas Oliver in 1770 or 1780. One of the latter dates appears the more probable. The one-story addition shown at the left is of recent date.

THE CROWINGSHIELD HOUSE AT DANVERSPORT, MASSACHUSETTS. (1798-1803.) Detail of Entrance.

The chaste simplicity and beauty of this entrance doorway and window overhead are well indicated in this picture. Indeed of all the three-story houses produced in this section, this dwelling seems to be the most perfectly proportioned, and at the same time the simplest, example.

191

THE KITTREDGE HOUSE, NORTH ANDOVER, MASSACHUSETTS.

Attributed to Samuel McIntyre, and very similar to the design of the Pierce-Nichols House in Salem, built by him in 1780 or 1782.   The same heavy detail and corner pilaster treatment are found in both structures.

GOVERNOR WOODBURY MANSION
NEAR PORTSMOUTH, NEW HAMPSHIRE.

Built in 1809 by Captain Samuel Ham.
Purchased by Levi Woodbury
(Governor of New Hampshire 1823–1824) in 1839.

One of the most unusually interesting—and also surprisingly little known—houses near Boston is the Baldwin house at Woburn, which is in some ways more pretentious and elaborate in treatment and detail than any other example of the three-story type to be found in the general vicinity of Boston. The siding of this house is entirely treated in imitation of the effect of stone divisions; the corner pilasters are given an entasis that is more nearly a "belly"; the architraves impinge upon a delicately moulded cornice; the roof balustrade is typical, in the refinement of its baluster shape and halving, of its comparatively old period; and finally, the entrance feature and Palladian window—while the former is somewhat injured by its extra width and both are in detail and size better suited to a two-story than a three-story type of house—yet remain nevertheless so interesting and suggestive for the architect as to make it nearly unique in importance among the treatments of this type of house to be found in New England.

At North Andover is an example of a McIntyre three-story house less well known than the example in Salem itself. McIntyre, when working on a house of this type, evidently followed his book very closely for his proportions and details,—the well-known refinement of his carving in mantelpieces and gate-posts and door-cap design is here laid aside for a sturdy and bold virility that is, under the circumstances, rather surprising. In this particular case an incidental defect is noted in the fact that, some time or other, the front columns of the entrance porch have been replaced by crudely turned shafts, and the bases of the former fluted columns have been utilized in place of the presumably exposed capitals. The balustrade here goes back to a break in the roof that suggests a monitor deck treatment: rather a more consistent and plausible location for this mode of roof adornment. The fence-posts of the gate at the rear of the house were brought from Salem to their present location, and are—as was of course to be expected!—also attributed to the much over-worked McIntyre.

The John Peirce house at Portsmouth is one of the well-known examples of this type of structure; and, despite the abominable entrance porch, its chaste simplicity and beauty of detail and moulding ornamentation amply serve to retain its interest for the student of good architecture.

THE CROWINGSHIELD HOUSE
DANVERSPORT, MASSACHUSETTS.

The porch and doorway, window caps and cornice help to relieve the square-ness of the design.

THE COLONEL LOAMMI BALDWIN HOUSE AT WOBURN, MASSACHUSETTS

The owner was an important and influential officer in the early Colonies and the discoverer and improver of the Baldwin apple. The half balusters and odd belly on the corner pilasters, along with their awkward height relation to the windows, are all to be noted in this view.

The very delicate detail shown in this picture and the small scale of the rusticated boarding seem inconsistent with the width of the entrance feature and the size of the whole house. The glass division is novel and unusual.

Simplest—and most beautiful—of all the houses of this type is the Boardman house at Portsmouth. Evidently the designer had merely in mind to carry out a design such as had been elsewhere used on a brick façade, substituting plank boarding for the other material, and at the same time greatly beautifying his whole composition by the charming grade, attenuation and refinement of the columns and pilasters in the curved porch and recessed Palladian window motif overhead. Such delicacy of moulding treatment and simplicity of design as are here shown would hardly be consistent with the heavier material and the larger scale of a brick dwelling,—but as it is, this house remains perhaps the most beautiful, chaste and distinguished instance of the Puritan treatment of this type of dwelling to be found in the New England colonies, and so should serve as epilogue and apogee to this brief record and appreciation of a type of Colonial dwelling unique and restricted to this section of North America.

THE JOHN PEIRCE HOUSE, COURT STREET, PORTSMOUTH, NEW HAMPSIRE. Built in 1799.

This house contains an excellent example of the old-fashioned circular staircase. The porch is a regrettable later addition. This design has been attributed by some to Bulfinch.

BOARDMAN HOUSE AT PORTSMOUTH, NEW HAMPSHIRE.

Built by Langley Boardman, an expert cabinetmaker, about 1800. The front hall, which was papered in 1816, shows scenes from Sir Walter Scott's "Lady of the Lake" and still appears in excellent condition. The front is treated with plain siding.

MANTELPIECE IN FRONT PARLOR
MAJ. ISRAEL FORSTER HOUSE—1804—MANCHESTER, MASSACHUSETTS

Early American Mantels

A T the time the fireplace was removed from its earlier location in the center of the room to one of its walls or corner angles, the square hearth shrank to a segment of its former area; and its marginal moulding seems, appropriately enough, to have extended upward over the wall surface in order to continue to limit the fireplace boundaries along its two sides and top. In those Mediæval days when the fire recess was first given an enclosed or concealed flue, it usually opened from the top of a stonebuilt hood, which itself soon became an appropriate part of the æsthetic design of the mantel, as well as exercising its inner functional purpose in collecting the smoke above the firebox and directing it into the flue that had been newly devised for the very practical purpose of removing the smoke from the room.

As the firebox itself became more deeply recessed into the wall—and especially as that wall became less a part of a stone built border castle and came into general use in the more humble dwelling of serf or retainer—the somewhat pretentious exterior hooded treatment disappeared from view; although it remained concealed more deeply within the wall, and was executed in humbler—and less fire resisting materials. In this less costly and more impermanent dwelling, the fireplace was either only partially built of stone inserted into a wooden or wattle wall,—or it largely or entirely filled one end of the principal room of the small dwelling; the flue often being carried up outside, of crisscrossed twigs heavily daubed with wet clay both inside and out.

This was also the earliest method employed in New England, and survivals of this treatment may still be found in early houses along the Eastern Coast, of which perhaps the best known examples are the early "stone-end" houses of New Jersey, Connecticut, and Rhode Island—or the brown stone dwellings of the lower Hudson Valley. When the house increased in size upon the ground, however, it became a matter of economy in construction, as well as in the conservation of heat and fuel, to place the chimney in the center of the small structure, thus enclosing the chimney and increasing the danger of fire, as well as bringing it between the inner walls of the two or three room floor plan. The chimney at once became larger, the fireplaces deeper, and the masonry construction of the fireplace itself came necessarily to be extended up through the wooden framed structure and well above its roof surfaces.

At the same time the fireplace began gradually to shrink in size, both in width—or length—height and depth. As this tendency continued, the æsthetic requirements of the owners (or perhaps it was only the woman's demand for simpler surfaces to clean and dust) introduced a wooden screen or partition that filled the remainder of these interior walls, separated the staircase and hall from the two or more rooms on each floor—and made necessary some sort of a boundary or lapping finish that would cover the point where the masonry fireplace stopped and the wood boarded wall at each side of and over it began. And so—and from quite another and different set of conditions—once again the suggestion for a moulded enframement of the fire opening evolved.

The danger of fire was still sufficient to require that the masonry firebox be extended in a facure upon both sides, and over the top of the fire opening, in the wall face; that the bordering woodwork be kept well back from the fire opening, and that a moulding be introduced to make tight the joint between the two materials and prevent any draft from drawing sparks up back of the paneling, into the space around and outside of the chimney flue. Among the earliest treatments, was the well known form of the "Bolection" moulding, at first used along the edge of the fire opening in stone, and later reproduced in wood (but at first still maintaining a full stone scale) four to eight inches back from the edge of the fire opening.

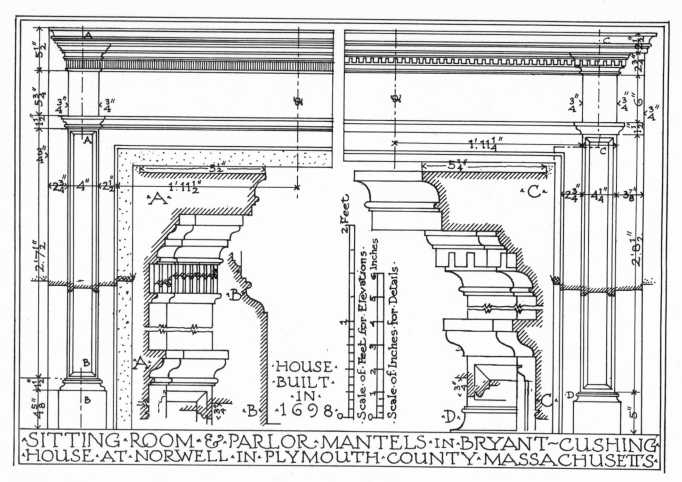

SITTING·ROOM·&·PARLOR·MANTELS·IN·BRYANT~CUSHING·
HOUSE·AT·NORWELL·IN·PLYMOUTH·COUNTY·MASSACHUSETTS·

HOUSE·
BUILT·
IN·
1698·

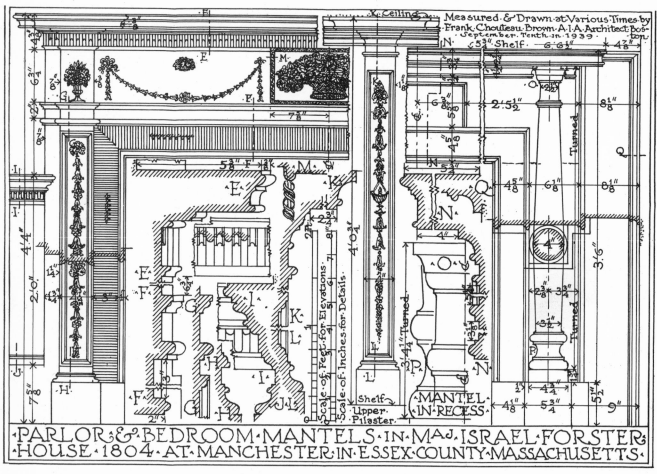

PARLOR·&·BEDROOM·MANTELS·IN·MAJ·ISRAEL·FORSTER·
HOUSE·1804·AT·MANCHESTER·IN·ESSEX·COUNTY·MASSACHUSETTS·

Measured·&·Drawn·at·Various·Times·by·
Frank·Chouteau·Brown·A·I·A·Architect·Bos-
ton·September·Tenth·in·1939·

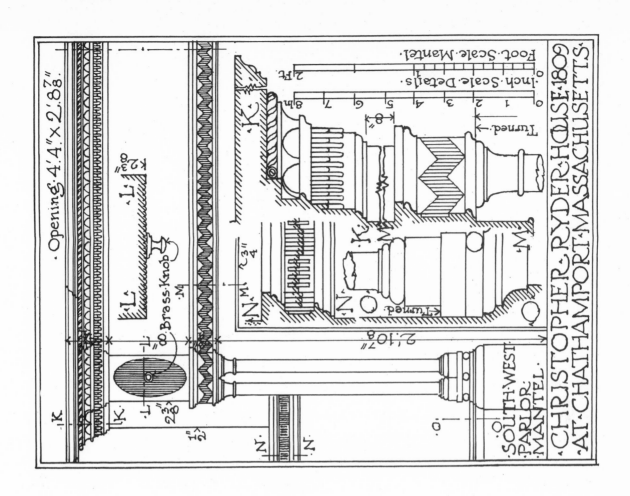

·Opening· 4'·4"× 2'·8.8".

·L·

2.3"

·L·

co.Brass·Knob·
·M·

Turned·

2'·10.7"

·SOUTH·WEST·
·PARLOR·
·MANTEL·

Foot·Scale·Mantel·
Inch·Scale·Details·
2 Ft.

8 in. 7 6 5 4 3 2 1

·CHRISTOPHER·RYDER·HOUSE·1809·
·AT·CHATHAMPORT·MASSACHUSETTS·

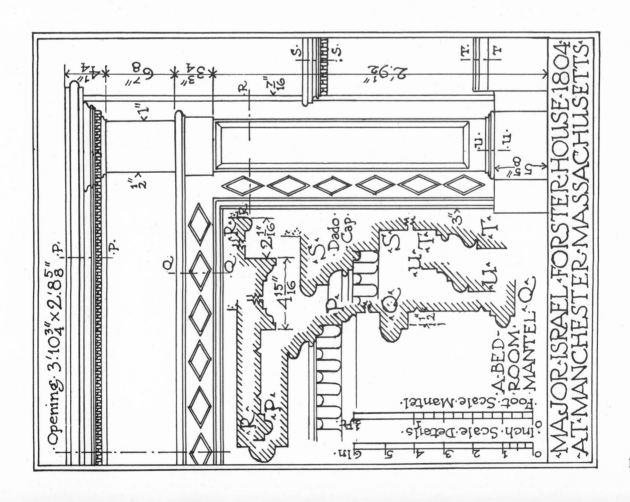

·Opening· 3'·10¾"× 2'·8.5" ·P·

·P·

·P·

·Q·

·Q·

Dado·
Cap·

·A·BED-
ROOM·
MANTEL·Q·

·S·

·T·

·U·

·U·

2'·9.2"

·T·

·T·

Foot·Scale·Mantel·
Inch·Scale·Details·
3 Ft.

6 in. 5 4 3 2 1

·MAJOR·ISRAEL·FORSTER·HOUSE·1804·
·AT·MANCHESTER·MASSACHUSETTS·

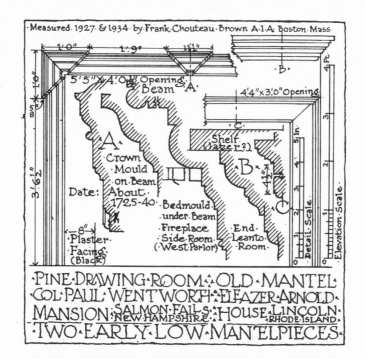

·Measured·1927·&·1934·by·Frank·Chouteau·Brown·A·I·A·Boston·Mass·

·PINE·DRAWING·ROOM· ·OLD·MANTEL·
·COL·PAUL·WENTWORTH· ·ELEAZER·ARNOLD·
·MANSION·SALMON·FALLS· ·HOUSE·LINCOLN·
·NEW·HAMPSHIRE· ·RHODE·ISLAND·
·TWO·EARLY·LOW·MANTELPIECES·

In some early fire-places this precaution was disregarded, and an example may be seen in the West Paneled Bedroom of the Wentworth Mansion.

This was a rather dangerous exception, nevertheless — as not only might sparks from the fire be carried in back of the paneling, but also the inner edge of the wood stiles come so near the edge of the masonry opening that the heat from a hot fire might easily start a conflagration.

In most cases, therefore, the early fireplaces in Colonial dwellings were placed back of a paneled end or side wall of a room, with a framing moulding around the fire opening. In other words, the rudiments of what is termed a "mantel." The earlier simple Bolection moulding, which often fitted back against the stile of a paneled wall treatment, was often aided by some especial emphasis on the area directly over the fireplace opening usually by a simple variation in the direction or arrangement of the panelwork itself.

A simple variant of the label moulding is often used without a shelf over it (although the latter is frequently added in later years — against a plain paneled wall in the earlier years, or — a little later — against a wall of plaster — as in the Oliver House. By early in the Eighteenth Century the use of plaster surfacing for at least three of the room walls became common, although the fireplace wall still continued to be paneled. The first change was to retain the high mantel with overpanel to the ceiling, sometimes with flanking side pilasters; but extending the plaster over the balance of the fourth wall, as well. This form was most typical of the English Georgian Period, and was fashionably followed in this country. But there being no longer a structural reason for the high mantel, it began by the end of the Century to disappear. The new fashion was to continue the lower portion of

OLD MANTEL
DR. PETER OLIVER HOUSE—1762
MIDDLEBOROUGH, MASSACHUSETTS

ELEAZER ARNOLD HOUSE—1687—LINCOLN, RHODE ISLAND

STEPHEN DANIEL HOUSE—1693—SALEM, MASSACHUSETTS

DETAILS OF FRIEZE AND PILASTER ORNAMENT, PARLOR MANTEL
MAJ. ISRAEL FORSTER HOUSE—1804—MANCHESTER, MASSACHUSETTS

the preceding form, with well established mantel shelf, and leave the wall space above it open for the hanging of a fine portrait or mirror.

An early example of this simple type is in the end-addition made to the Eleazer Arnold House —a dwelling which is also one of the best examples of the Rhode Island "stone-end" fireplace house plan.

Another simple example is in the Col. John Gorham House. This is the type that has continued a favorite down to the present day. Embellished, as it has been, by small pilasters, by carved panels and frieze decorations, by carpenter's hand worked and chiseled grooves, by varied and flowing outlines, it is the type to which the other illustrations in this issue have been given.

Two early examples of the new pilaster supports are in the Bryant-Cushing House. An example of a transitional type from the preceding "over-mantel panel," is shown; where two delicate pilasters extend from the lower mantel shelf to the cornice of the room. The influence of Samuel McIntire is clearly evident in this mantel,—and, as Maj. Forster came from Marblehead to settle in Manchester, there may be reason for this resemblance—

CHRISTOPHER RYDER HOUSE, 1809, CHATHAMPORT, MASSACHUSETTS

DETAILS OF CARVING, McINTIRE MANTEL, THE "LINDENS," FORMERLY AT DANVERS, MASSACHUSETTS
TAKEN FROM THE NATHAN READ HOUSE—1790—DEMOLISHED IN SALEM, 1856

although its charming delicacy contrasts strongly with the bedroom mantel.

Incidentally, the wall paper on this parlor was ordered by the owner from England, and, along with papers on the Dr. Oliver, and Samuel Fowler rooms, show five early examples in this issue. Another McIntire mantel is the sole survivor of the Salem over-door and three mantels from the Nathan Read House (Salem, 1790) that were installed in the "Lindens" by Francis Peabody on his purchase of the place in 1860—even against its incongruous 1754 paneled breasts!

In the Samuel Fowler mantels, reappear the same local hand-cut and turned "carpenter patterns," to which notice was directed in the details of the doorways.

Equal ingenuity is displayed by Cape Cod workmen at the Christopher Ryder House at Chathamport, who, with their grooved chisels, worked otherwise plain surfaces into partially fluted and beaded treatments.

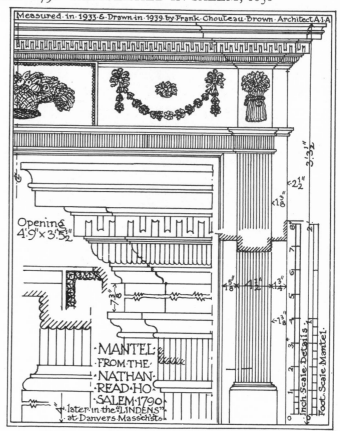

Measured in 1933 & Drawn in 1939 by Frank Chouteau Brown Architect A.I.A

Opening 4'9" x 3'5½"

MANTEL FROM THE NATHAN READ HO. SALEM 1790
later in the "LINDENS" at Danvers Massch'sts

Dining Room Mantel
COL. JOHN GORHAM HOUSE—1690—BARNSTABLE, MASS.

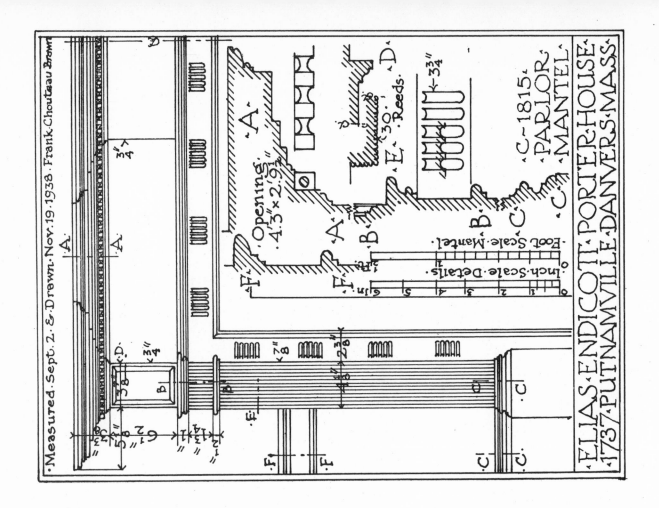

·ELIAS·ENDICOTT·PORTER·HOUSE·
·1737·PUTNAMVILLE·DANVERS·MASS·

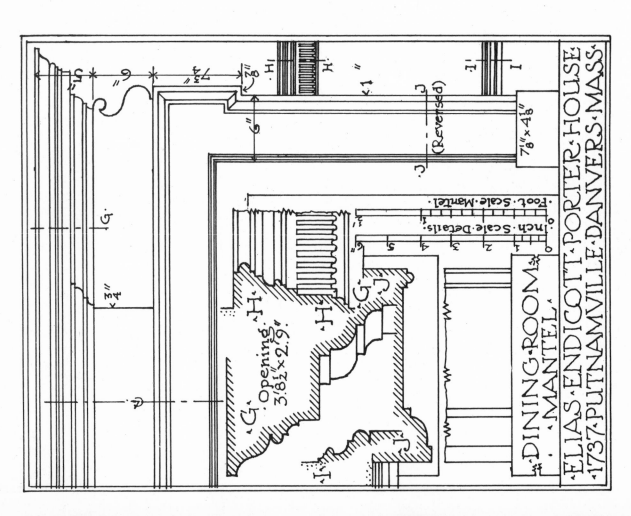

·ELIAS·ENDICOTT·PORTER·HOUSE·
·1737·PUTNAMVILLE·DANVERS·MASS·

Kitchen Fireplace and Mantel

OLD TAVERN INN—C. 1700—SOUTH MIDDLEBOROUGH, MASSACHUSETTS

ELIAS ENDICOTT PORTER FARMHOUSE—1737—DANVERS, MASSACHUSETTS

CIRCULAR TOPPED WINDOW ON STAIRCASE LANDING
"THE LINDENS"—1754—FORMERLY AT DANVERS, MASSACHUSETTS

Interior Views of Early American Windows

IN the North American colonies, the "double-hung" type of window came into use gradually from shortly after the beginning of the Eighteenth Century. We have knowledge of structures, built in the first years after 1700, with the casement framed sash still in use, probably by about 1720 to 1735 the newer double-hung sash style had been generally accepted, and the older buildings were being gradually changed over to agree with the new English fashion.

By then, too, many of the Glassworks on the new continent were becoming proficient enough to manufacture window glass that, while it still contained many imperfections in thickness and surface, was yet becoming commercially available in sizes that were growing gradually larger and clearer during the balance of that century until—by the early years of the Nineteenth—glass areas as large as 12 x 15 to 12 x 18 inches were in common use. By that time, too, the usually proportioned window openings were customarily being fitted with two sash, each probably having six lights, thus filling the entire opening with twelve lights of glass, three wide and four high. This arrangement and proportion continued to be employed until well into the latter half of that century, when windows having only four—or even, finally, but two—glazed areas, came into the market.

But with the period with which we are now concerned—the hundred years extending from about 1720 to 1820—the double-hung sash window was gradually increasing in its dimensions, along with the gradually enlarging rooms of the "Georgian" house, and the considerably higher ceilings that were then coming into vogue. In many cases the older dwellings, into which these new window frames were being built, had not previously been finished inside other than by walls faced with "feather edged" boards, even if they had not even been left without any inside surface finish whatever, as had often been the case with the first built structures. It was, therefore, compara-

tively easy to insert the new window frames, with their two sliding sash, and then—or a little later—refinish the entire interior with the different styles of paneled walls and dadoes; or the plaster walls and ceilings that were then beginning to be copied from the more imposing mansions of Georgian England. And this inner plaster facing, when it was added, could as easily be furred in some eight or ten more inches, thus completely concealing the heavy upright corner posts still found in the house framing and at the same time setting the window within a recess, the sloping and paneled reveals of which were in many cases the very shutters closing over the opening, now arranged to fold back upon either side when not in use. These shutters took the place of those that had previously hung exposed, as in the Short House or slid back into the space at one or both sides of the window opening, as in the Wentworth house.

The very earliest and simplest type of double-hung window is, perhaps, only represented by the single example of the dormer treatment shown upon the next page. In the small early cottage, the nicest possible adjustment of harmony in scale and composition is essential for their successful employment, both within and without the building. No attempt has been made, in this issue, to cover other than the usual window usage, save in a couple of examples of stairway landing windows, both employing an arched, or semi-circular, top. One is from the Sarah Orne Jewett House, and the other, from the somewhat more pretentious "Lindens," formerly at Danvers, Massachusetts.

In other cases, this central Second Hall window is only marked by being somewhat shorter or longer than others with which it lines upon the house exterior, except in those cases where it provides an outlet, perhaps, upon a porch roof or balcony, as happens with the example from the Woodbridge-Short House, at Salem where the third sash was introduced to obtain the length necessary for that purpose.

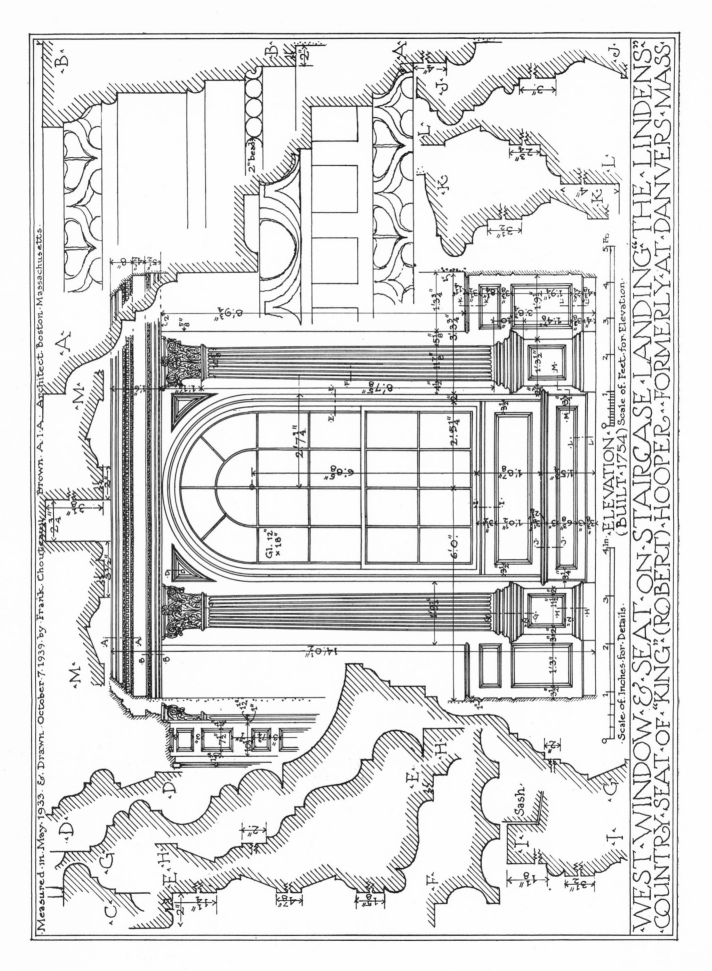

·WEST·WINDOW·&·SEAT·ON·STAIRCASE·LANDING·THE·"LINDENS"
·COUNTRY·SEAT·OF·"KING"·(ROBERT)·HOOPER·FORMERLY·AT·DANVERS·MASS·

·ELEVATION·
·(BUILT·1754)· Scale·of·Feet·for·Elevation·

Scale·of·Inches·for·Details·

·Measured·in·May·1933·&·Drawn·October·7·1939·by·Frank·Chouteau·Brown·A·I·A·Architect·Boston·Massachusetts·

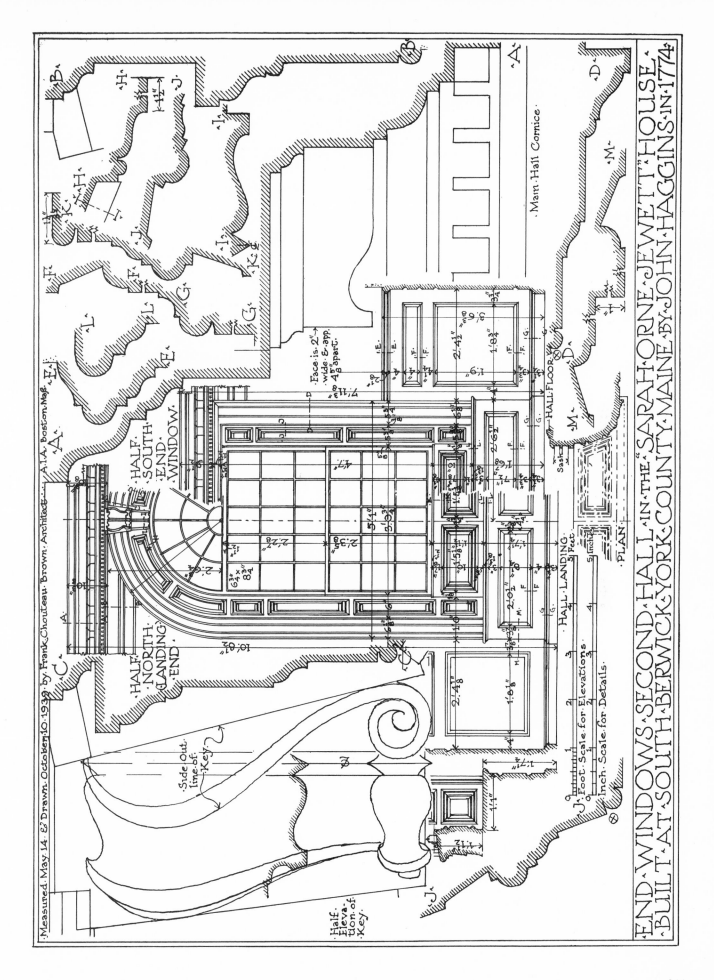

END·WINDOWS·SECOND·HALL·IN·THE·"SARAH·ORNE·JEWETT"·HOUSE·
·BUILT·AT·SOUTH·BERWICK·YORK·COUNTY·MAINE·BY·JOHN·HAGGINS·IN·1774·

Measured·May·14·&·Drawn·October·10·1939·by·Frank·Chouteau·Brown·Architect·A.I.A.·Boston·Mass·

·HALF·SOUTH·END·WINDOW·

·HALF·NORTH·LANDING·END·

·Main·Hall·Cornice·

·Hall·Landing·

·Plan·

·Half·Elevation·of·Key·

·Side·Out·line·of·Key·

Foot·Scale·for·Elevations.

Inch·Scale·for·Details.

A considerable part of the interior effectiveness of these windows depended upon the importance of their molded or recessed framing. In earlier and simpler examples this was often very slight—sometimes the wooden reveal of the opening ended only with a beaded edge, left projecting slightly beyond the plaster wall face. Often the facing was widened by another strip of molded finish. Sometimes this framing of the window opening was extended down to the floor below or connected with the cornice above. In the first case, a different panel of woodwork, or perhaps a seat fitted into the recess, might fill the space beneath the window. Or the bottom of the window might line with the top of a plain wooden dado carried about the room or even break down into a higher dado, to fit into its paneled arrangement. Where the window trim did not merely cope into the cornice above; where it was mitred across over the top of the opening, or brought up against the under side of the cornice with an intermediate frieze; the cornice might be broken out to mark more distinctly the window location. It was then often broken out in a similar manner over a door, or mantel, upon another side of the room, even when it had no actual physical connection with either one.

All this emphasis of the interior architectural framing of the window opening was a gradual development that accompanied the greater wealth of the new builders and owners of homes in the principal coastal cities of the Colonies, but still did not much affect the continuing use of the simpler, earlier forms of double-hung windows in the smaller villages, cottages, and farmhouses of the countryside. There the older low ceilings continued in use, and the smaller scaled glass areas that were relative to their more modest dimensions continued to be employed; and so the smaller glass sizes were carried along in use up to a comparatively late time, just as they were, during the same period, gradually increasing in size and diminishing

INTERIOR OF RECESSED DORMER WINDOW
"HOUSE AT HEAD OF THE COVE"—BEFORE 1750—
ANNISQUAM, MASSACHUSETTS

in number, in the larger and more pretentious dwellings of pre-Revolutionary and Revolutionary times.

In the illustration showing the window and curtaining from a chamber in the Concord Antiquarian House, the window, which is glazed with twenty-four small lights, does not extend to touch the McIntire type cornice at the top of the wall, although it is treated in the manner characteristic of his work of about 1810-11 in Salem—even though there usually employed in rooms of more ample height. The recess and the side architraves framing the opening are carried down to the floor below. The bottom of the window still lines with the top of the plain dado design, but the space above the window panel under the opening (which also lines in height with the cap of the dado) is enriched with a jig-sawn pattern applied upon the wood back—as was so often

TWENTY-FOUR-LIGHT WINDOW IN FIRST STORY ROOM

SHORT HOUSE—C. 1732—OLD NEWBURY, MASSACHUSETTS

woven fabric that was known as "India muslin" in the time of Sheraton, from whom this treatment has been adapted.

In addition to providing examples of their architectural treatment, and showing the window opening in relation to its surrounding wall areas, as the illustrations have been selected to do, a certain number also indicate some of the several methods and styles of curtaining that are appropriate to the different periods of their design. As a general rule, it might be stated that in a house of any authentic Colonial period, the simpler the decorative treatment the more successful and satisfying is generally the result. This applies especially to the selection and arrangement of the drapery in or about the window openings.

If too heavy, it destroys the proportion and structural framing of the opening, as well as obscures the light. If too light, it may appear skimpy or meagre; although under rather than over-elaboration is always to be preferred! Some windows, especially of the earlier periods, are the better for the omission of colored curtaining altogether. And, above all, nothing so quickly and entirely destroys the directness

McIntire's custom with his decoration, whether sawn or carved—as it may be seen in the Woodbridge-Short and Pingree, or other of the houses in Salem of his later design.

The curtaining of this window, while it entirely hides all the enframing wooden trim about the recessed opening (rather a pity, when well conceived and proportioned!) is yet nevertheless to be approved for its restraint in pattern and arrangement. As shown here it is made of a plain dusty blue stuff, velvet-like in quality, and sufficiently thin to take pleasant folds where back-tied with strips of the same velvet. It hangs from behind a formal boxed heading of the material, emphasized by a braided outline, while it is set off by an equally simple pair of muslin sash curtains (often advisedly omitted in formal Georgian rooms of heavier design), suggesting the sheer

and dignity of formal early American interiors, as an over-draped and eccentric arrangement of the material —except perhaps the use of over-emphasized and incongruous brocaded patterns, or an over brilliant and glaring color contrast, either in the material or with the walls and color scheme otherwise dominating the room. Even the most elaborately detailed authentic Georgian interiors of pre-Revolutionary date are usually much bettered by the simplest of window curtaining, or equally injured by the addition of unnecessary fripperies. Particularly in these days, when careful analysis and research are disclosing that white was neither invariably the original paint color applied over the interior trim, nor paper even the usual original treatment of the walls! We now know that later fashions have covered a mass of early coloring on walls and woodwork.

SARAH ORNE JEWETT HOUSE—1774—SO. BERWICK, MAINE

BEZALEEL MANN HOUSE—1790—NORTH ATTLEBOROUGH,
MASSACHUSETTS

GEN. SALEM TOWNE HOUSE—1796—CHARLTON,
MASSACHUSETTS

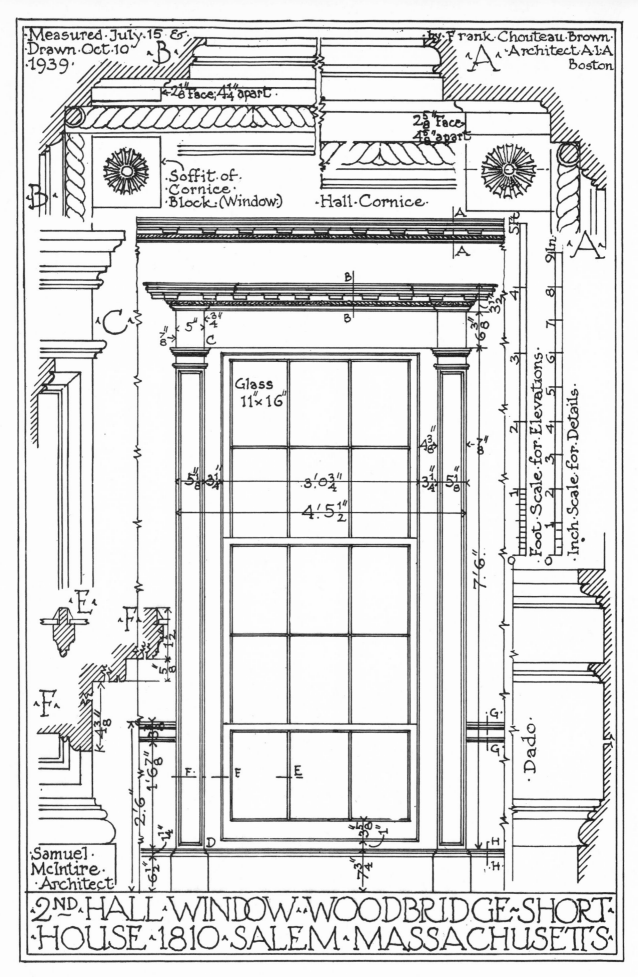

Measured July 15 &
Drawn Oct 10
1939

by Frank Chouteau Brown
Architect A.I.A
Boston

B

A

2⅞" face; 4¼" apart

2⅝" face
4⅝" apart

Soffit of
Cornice
Block (Window)

Hall Cornice

B

A

C

Glass
11"×16"

3'0¾"

4'5½"

7'6"

Foot Scale for Elevations

Inch Scale for Details

Dado

E

F

F

Samuel
McIntire
Architect

2'6"

1'6⅞"

Samuel McIntire Architect

2ND·HALL·WINDOW·WOODBRIDGE·SHORT·
HOUSE·1810·SALEM·MASSACHUSETTS

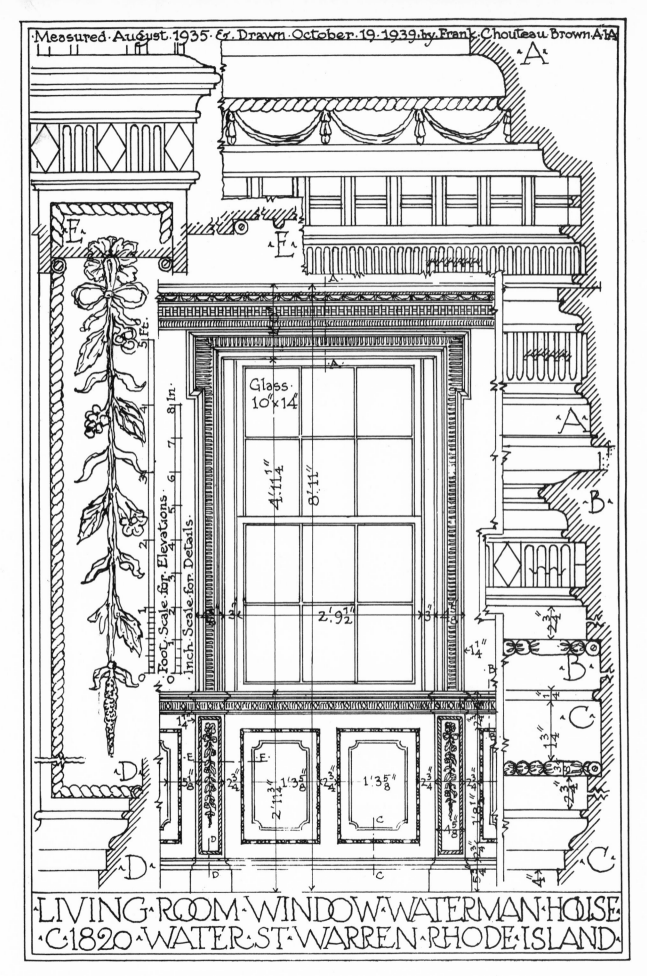

Glass·
10"×14"

4'.11¼"

8'.11"

2'.9½"

5·Ft.

8·In.

7

6

5

4

3

2

1

0

Foot·Scale·for·Elevations

Inch·Scale·for·Details.

2'.11¼"

1'.3⅝"

1'.3⅝"

LIVING·ROOM·WINDOW·WATERMAN·HOUSE·
C·1820·WATER·ST·WARREN·RHODE·ISLAND·

217

WOODBRIDGE-SHORT HOUSE—1810—SALEM, MASSACHUSETTS

WATERMAN HOUSE—C. 1820—WARREN, RHODE ISLAND

RICHARD DERBY HOUSE—1761—DERBY STREET, SALEM,
MASSACHUSETTS

COL. PAUL WENTWORTH MANSION—1701—SALMON FALLS,
NEW HAMPSHIRE

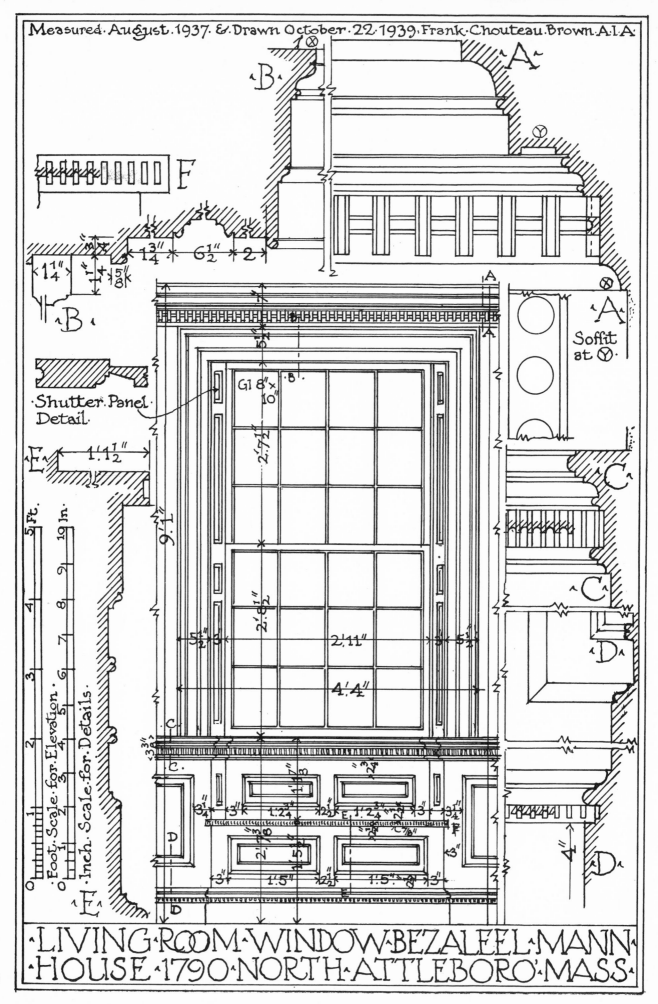

Measured · August · 1937 · & · Drawn · October · 22 · 1939 · Frank · Chouteau · Brown · A.I.A.

·B·
·A·

F

1 3/4″   6 1/2″   2

·B·

Shutter · Panel
Detail.

G1 8″ x 10″

Soffit
at ⊗.

·A·

·C·

2'.7 1/2″

9'.1″

E

1'.1 1/2″

2'.8 1/2″

2'.11″

4'.4″

·C·

·D·

Shutter Panel Detail.

5 1/2″   5 1/2″

3″

1'.4 3/4″   2 1/4″

3/4″   3″   1'.2 4″   2 1/2″   E. 1'.2 3/4″   2 4″   3″   1 3/4″   4″   ·D·

2'.3 5/8″   1.5 3/8″   C 3/8″

3″   1'.5″   2 1/2″   1'.5″   3″

Foot · Scale · for · Elevation.   Inch · Scale · for · Details.

·E·

·LIVING·ROOM·WINDOW·BEZALEEL·MANN·
HOUSE·1790·NORTH·ATTLEBORO·MASS·

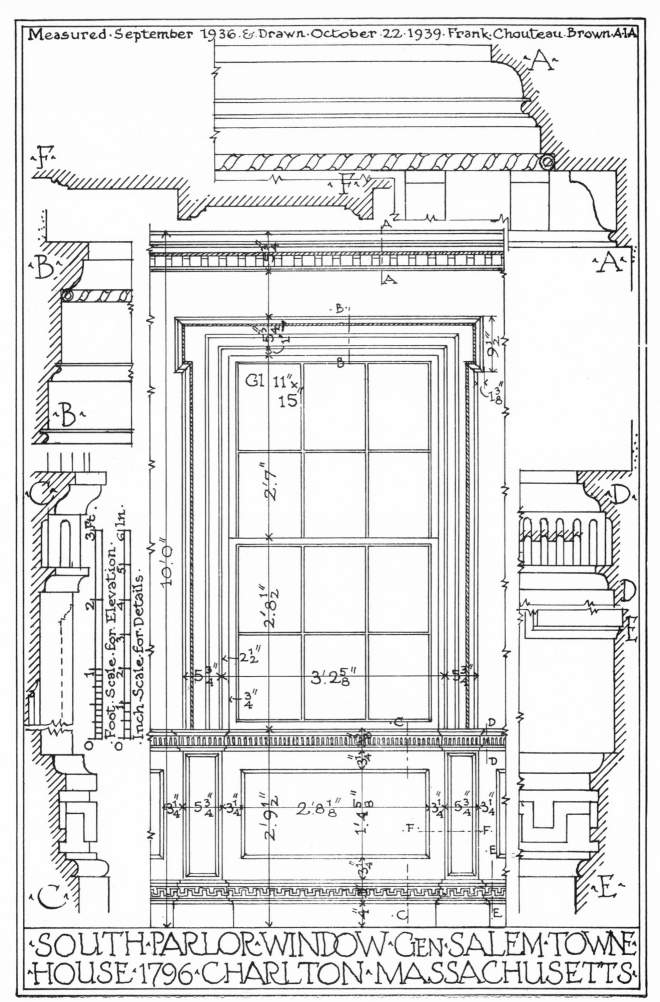

~A~

~F~

~B~

~B~

~C~

3·Ft.

·Foot·Scale·For·Elevation·

·Inch·Scale·for·Details·

10'·0"

~A~

A

~A~

·B·

B

Gl 11"x 15

9½"

1 3/8"

2'·7"

~D~

D

D

2'·8½"

2½"

5¾"

3'·2 5/8"

5¾"

3/4"

C

D

C

D

3¾"

2'·9½"

3¼" 5¾" 3¼"

2'·8 1/8"

1'·4 5/8"

3¼" 5¾" 3¼"

F

F

E

3¼"

~E~

4"

C

E

~C~

·SOUTH·PARLOR·WINDOW·Gen·SALEM·TOWNE·
HOUSE·1796·CHARLTON·MASSACHUSETTS·

FIFTEEN-LIGHT WINDOWS IN PARLOR END, LATER PORTION
ELIAS ENDICOTT PORTER FARMHOUSE—C. 1815—DANVERS, MASSACHUSETTS

WINDOWS IN SOUTH CHAMBER
HOUSE OF JOHN TURNER ("SEVEN GABLES")—1668—SALEM, MASSACHUSETTS

Twenty-Four-Light Window, and Draperies, of Early Nineteenth Century
ANTIQUARIAN HOUSE, CONCORD, MASSACHUSETTS